Radical Youth Work

Developing Critical Perspectives and Professional Judgement

Brian A. Belton

'The difference between ⟨...⟩ but someone or something ha⟨...⟩ ⟨...⟩ ⟨...⟩ ⟨...⟩ the best way to do that is to prese⟨...⟩ ⟨...⟩eone with the unexpected ... something that for whatever reason draws them in.'

Vic Emery, Canadian Olympic Bobsled Team Gold Medallist

RHP

Russell House Publishing

Russell House Publishing
First published in 2010 by:
Russell House Publishing Ltd
4 St George's House
Uplyme Road
Lyme Regis
Dorset DT7 3LS

Tel: 01297-443948
Fax: 01297-442722
e-mail: help@russellhouse.co.uk

www.russellhouse.co.uk

British Library Cataloguing-in-publication Data:
A catalogue record for this book is available from the British Library.

ISBN: 978-1-905541-57-7

Typeset by TW Typesetting, Plymouth, Devon

Printed by Page Bros

Russell House Publishing

Russell House Publishing aims to publish innovative and valuable materials to
help managers, practitioners, trainers, educators and students.
Our full catalogue covers: social policy, working with young people, helping
children and families, care of older people, social care, combating social
exclusion, revitalising communities and working with offenders.

Full details can be found at www.russellhouse.co.uk and we are pleased to send
out information to you by post. Our contact details are on this page.

We are always keen to receive feedback on publications and new ideas for future
projects.

Dedication

Bishop Roger Sainsbury – who at the Mayflower, Canning Town, had faith in my potential as a young person and in so doing demonstrated to me the essence of what it is to be an effective youth worker.

All the royalties from this book will be donated to Great Ormond Street Hospital

The true teacher defends their pupils against his/her own personal influence.
S/he inspires self-distrust.
S/he guides their eyes from him/herself to the spirit that quickens him/her.
S/he will have no disciple.

Amos Bronson Alcott

Contents

Foreword

Writing a foreword for a book which does not seek disciples is a fairly exquisite challenge. When the book is the work of my colleague, Brian Belton, it is all the harder to resist the temptation of the challenge.

I am not a disciple of this book. It is annoying, opinionated, impossible, persuasive, affectionate and, in my own partial opinion, sometimes wrong. It scratches my sense of curiosity and inquiry where it itches – but fails absolutely to ease it. It is demanding of my time without recompense. Indeed, the more time I give it, the more time it grabs and devours. It insinuates itself under my professional skin and disturbs my certainty, sometimes gently, sometimes brutally – ever insistently. So, why bother? As Brian asks, what can we do?

I am using this foreword to propose that we can do three things. We can read the book – but I would warn against the cover to cover approach. And here the reader's usual accolade – I could not put this book down – fails utterly. This is a book which has to be put down to allow us to measure up the arguments against our experience. It takes time for us to disturb our taken-for-granted thinking and make space for the iconoclastic, the amusing and the unwelcoming insights which the book requires us to entertain.

We can reply in the spirit of its author – in a constructive, and a radical, tongue. And here the title introduces us to a world in which there is a consistent interplay between the practical and the intellectual. Building – the practical, dirty handed and visible construction of – radical theory. We can read the book in order to build the means to burrow down into the root of the matter: to engage in the process of opening up possibilities. We can dig deep into our professional mantras because a radical shake-up offers us a robust (if painful) foundation for thought.

We can respond to the paradox the book offers – to read with scepticism in order to enlighten ourselves; to mistrust the guide when we will, while holding absolute confidence in our journey together. Like that of TS Eliot's Magi, there is something of 'a hard time' in this journey which takes us from education through to consideration, from colonialism to conviviality. In following that journey, I was *moved* into a place which recognised the value of logical inquiry suffused with emotional integrity. The book asks us to travel from head towards heart – a direction which comes from Belton's humane engagement with the world in which we find ourselves. The author's sense of respect – and of affection – for youth work and for youth workers is always worthwhile and always present. 'Our honour as workers is that we might have the time and hopefully the ability to be with people as they become what they need and want to be; to stand with them and by them and have them stand by us.' This seam of affection – for the work and the workers, for fellow writers and their books – leads Belton to share his life story and his passion. In his hands, radical discourses emerge from their traditional politically correct silos – and become genuinely radical – because they require us to engage whole-heartedly in the adventures of creative thought.

Brian Belton and I have worked together for most of the past twenty years. In working with him, I have come to predict the unexpected. I have rarely, if ever, ended a conversation with Brian without feeling the interesting discomfort of some surprising new insight. I sense that this book, in its turn, will leave readers with an academic hair shirt of doubt and curiosity. This morning, as we started a discussion about a student's writing, our conversation wandered through the importance of opening opportunities, to balancing diverse process with equal outcomes, via new technologies, Berkeley's Hotel and the Scotch Malt Whisky Club. This book leads us through Brian's own life and work by way of Chomsky, Uruguay, *Matrix* and Marx. It cannot, necessarily, be a book of answers but nor is it simply one of questions. For me, what makes the book radical is the apparent ease with which the author hands back the thinking to where it belongs for each one of us: to the reader. That is the kernel which reminds us of the enormous and radical possibilities of youth work – the intellectual stance which shares thinking and concluding in a spirit of mutual engagement and effort. That is why I hope this book will be read by youth workers as much as by teachers and social workers. It will support work with young people by supporting the workers and by focussing our attention clearly on the fruitful moment where our work blossoms in the light of our thinking. And, what price must the reader be willing to pay? The price – and the prize – of an authentic and critical evaluation of what we are doing: 'If you don't reconsider your practice it is likely that you haven't really read this book.'

Mary Wolfe
Principal
YMCA George Williams College
2009

About the Author and the Contributors

Dr. Brian Belton was born and bred in the West Ham/Canning Town area of London. Brian's father, the son of a Gypsy mother and a gas works stoker father, was a stall holder (costermonger) and his mother, a former school dinner lady, is the daughter of an East London socialist councillor who played an active role in the radical Popularism movement of the 1920s.

After finishing his initial education at Burke Secondary Modern School in Plaistow, Brian started his working life alongside his father. He graduated from the East End youth gang culture of the late 1960s and early 1970s, to take up professional training in youth and community work. After practicing as a youth worker in Bethnal Green he attended City University to gain his BSc. Working with some of the most challenging young people in locations as diverse as Glasgow and the Falkland Islands, Brian completed his Masters degree at Essex University and was awarded his Doctorate by the University of Kent in 2000 (his thesis focused on the nature of identity, race and ethnicity).

Brian is now a senior lecturer at the YMCA George Williams College in Canning Town and an experienced author, sociologist, critical anthropologist and social historian.

Brian has written close to 40 books (several focusing on his beloved West Ham United Football Club), including: *Questioning Gypsy Identity: Ethnic Narratives in Britain and America*, AltaMira (2004): *Gypsy and Traveller Ethnicity: The Social Generation of an Ethnic Phenomenon*, Routledge (2004): *Black Hammers: The Voices of West Ham's Ebony Heroes*, Pennant Books (2006); *A Dream Come True: Lewis Hamilton*, Pennant Books (2007): *Fay Taylour. Queen of Speedway*, Panther (2006).

YMCA George Williams College is the biggest trainer of youth workers in the UK (at any one time they have about 800 students on course at post pre-graduate and undergraduate levels all over the UK). Brian is responsible for two courses on the College's undergraduate programme where this book will be used.

Brian has taught and been involved in youth work all over the world and is well known in that profession and across the YMCA (the largest youth movement across the globe). In any one year he comes into contact with hundreds of youth workers and their managers/employers and over his long career he has been involved with thousands of people developing their careers in the field, from in-service training and pre-graduate course to Masters level and PhD study.

Tania de St Croix has been involved in youth work, play schemes and community activism since leaving school in 1993. She grew up in Bath and has mostly lived and worked there and in Manchester. She is currently a detached youth worker for a small charity in Hackney, London. Tania is a committed and energetic environmentalist.

Zuber Ahmed has worked in several voluntary youth and community organisations in a range of settings, from detached youth work to conventional youth club environments and has also been involved with several international youth programmes. He is presently employed by Tower Hamlets Youth Service, as a senior youth worker, managing a youth centre and a team of staff. (A fuller account of Zuber's background and experience can be found at the start of the *Conclusion* that is his contribution to this book.)

Introduction

This book is devoted to the development of professional judgement and political perspective within the youth and community work profession. The ideas, theories and standpoints included are deployed as much needed examples of critique in a field that has become moribund. This situation has had, with hindsight, predictable consequences. Over the last two decades youth work has become increasingly eroded by state attempts to make professional interaction with young people outside school more effective in terms of the implementation of government policy and the resulting organisational aims. Practice has more and more mirrored and confirmed state strategies in line with the requirements of funding and the need to adhere to requisite legislation. This is a shift in focus from individuals and groups of young people and their personal and collective perspectives, to functional economic requirements at a national level. Youth work outcomes now have a skills priority based on the requirements of creating a relatively flexible, relatively cheap workforce with the aim of making Britain more competitive within the international capitalist labour market. At the same time the emphasis in youth work has been placed on notions embedded in forms of individual development. This is often framed within particular political ideals and psychological theory, having moved away from understanding that the strength of young people is their relatively unmediated potential as a fresh and vibrant natural resource to reinvigorate and shape society. These shifts have created a collective attempt to make 'them' more like 'us'. Traditionally it was understood that 'they' would eventually replace 'us' with what 'they' are. However, wanting them to *replicate* 'us' is not only folly, likely to incite righteous rebellion, but socially regressive.

The purpose of this book

As such, this work is concerned with subjecting the current practice paradigm (and by implication practitioners) associated ideas and what passes as theory, to positive critical analysis. In this sense the material brought together in this book seeks to help those in the field generate 'radical' practice theory; it looks to provide a basis, a launching pad for individual practitioners, via their professional judgement, to alter perceptions and delivery routines of services. This draws on the interpretation of notion of basic radicalism as arising from or going to a root or source. However, aligning with the way the word is often used in education the radicalism that this book seeks to provoke is a marked departure from what has become the usual or accepted ways of thinking about or interpreting youth work. Tania de St Croix discusses radicalism further on pages 60–83.

The nature and role of radicalism

For all this, as the title suggests, no book or collection of words can be radical in themselves. Radical theory may be able to be realised in practice, but this animation can only be engendered by those engaged in face to face work. However, for practice to be continuingly radical it needs to give rise to the development and maintenance of 'critical perspectives' that are themselves realised in the practice of professional judgement. The pages that follow might be understood as providing some material, inspiration or motivation that might ignite, reinvigorate or confirm, potential, budding, evolving or lapsed youth work radicals to acquire or to continue to hone critical perspectives and, premised on this, assert their professional judgement – what I believe to be the 'source and root' of radical theory.

As you can discern, this is something of a self-reinforcing cycle: radical theory is enlivened via practice, the critique of which provides the basis and provocation of professional judgment (development or even the rejection of convention) that is the conduit of radical theory (that tested in practice evokes further critique).

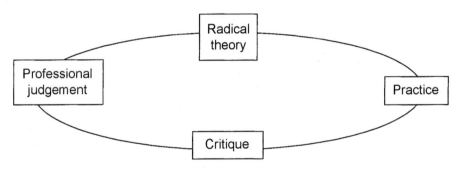

Figure 1 The radical theory cycle

Politics, education and communities

So, as might now be clear, this is not a 'how to' handbook. There are quite enough informal education youth work handbooks and text books on the market that reflect the relative political neutrality of the field and most of the initial training for the profession. This has produced practitioners who preach and extol 'democracy' but who are in the main politically naïve. For example, many youth workers now see their role as entwined with 'community education' and as such understand themselves to be 'educators' first and foremost. However, an appreciable number of youth workers on graduation struggle to provide a clear statement about the social function and political purpose of 'education' in the context of contemporary Western society beyond declaring that education is about 'promoting positive activities' and making 'informed judgements'. It is unclear how it is decided what 'positive' might be: or who controls or formulates the information provided for the making of judgements. An often heard maxim is that 'education is a contested arena'. This in itself is something of a misnomer. Straightforwardly, for most intents and purposes, education is the acquisition of knowledge and the means of acquiring knowledge is learning; education is a train bound for the destination of knowledge on the track of learning. This being the case, the outcomes of education can, and always have been, measurable (via qualifications, exams etc.). Awareness, reflection, imagination, revelation, dreams, epiphany, feelings, illusions, thoughts and so on are not of themselves education, they are in the main subjective experiences that might provide insight and together with education wisdom. Or they might not, in that they can serve to delude us about the nature of objective reality – this was partly the point Descartes was making in his *Discourse on Method*.

What *is* contested however is what 'knowledge' should be learned and taught and how this knowledge might be differentiated from propaganda and indoctrination.

At the same time, it appears that the nature of the site of youth work practice, the community, can be something of a mystery even to experienced practitioners given the sometimes largely incoherent responses one can be offered when asking what community might be. The equally enigmatic, hackneyed surrogate notion of 'neighbourhood' is sometimes deployed to somehow explain what community might be, but to say 'a community is a neighbourhood' just leads to what is more or less the same question; 'what is a neighbourhood?' At this point it is not unusual to be involved in a conversation about geography, peppered with vague references to the Black/Asian/Gay (and etc.) communities, whose boundaries seem to be restricted to the neighbourhood or alternatively almost totally unlimited. The Asian community for example seemingly being an all inclusive group of Bengalis, Pakistanis, Indians, Sri Lankans and occasionally Iraqis and Iranians amongst others.

Hence it is not unusual to find professionals claiming to do something they don't understand within a social entity they cannot describe beyond what the proverbial person 'on the Clapham omnibus' might recite.

Being curious about education

This situation is not the fault of youth workers, but it does reflect the banality of many of the texts that claim to inform practitioners. At the same time, the work circumstances that many youth workers find themselves dealing with is, in their every day functioning, concerned with forms of 'protection' (surveillance) 'welfare' (child care) 'management' (administrative fire fighting) and pretty much formalised (didactic) instruction and advice giving. These work conditions do little to provoke research into, or the engendering of inquisitiveness about, education.

Therefore this book is concerned more with 'why' and 'what' than 'how', although practical suggestions are included. I have sought to at least begin to tackle the current paucity of critique of current ideas relating to youth work. Although around 60,000 words are never going to be enough, I hope that this book will at least motivate, provoke and inspire a greater curiosity about the structures and forces that support our practice and the questions that pop out of the realm almost constantly. For example, as long ago as 1990 the Minister of Education in Scotland approved the following definition of community education, against which functional analysis for community educators was carried out in that country, so laying the foundation for community education practice. It should help set the scene for the book:

Community education is a process designed to enrich the lives of individuals and groups by engaging with people living within a geographical area, or sharing a common interest, to develop voluntarily a range of learning, action, and reflection opportunities determined by their personal, social, economic and political needs.

The function role of the community educator in society, therefore, is that of an animateur, positively intervening and engaging with people within their community, motivating, organising and enthusing them to acquire new knowledge, skills and confidence. In Scotland this has been closely linked to community development strategies for tackling social exclusion, for supporting individual and community enterprise and self-help and for encouraging public participation in determining change.

First of all, who decided that people needed their lives 'enriched'? The assumption in this is that people are relatively impoverished and that this needs seeing to. Who decides on what form this 'enrichment' might take? How will it be decided when someone needs 'enrichment' or when they have had enough 'enriching'? The provision of 'learning, action and reflection opportunities' suggests that these do not exist without the provision of community education. What evidence is this based on?

What constitutes 'positive intervention'? One person's 'positive' is another's 'negative'. Who defines what or where the 'community' is? Why is there an assumption that people require 'motivating, organising and enthusing'? This is another set of assumptions that people are relatively demotivated, disorganised and apathetic. Once more the question is begged, on what are these assumptions based? Community education it seems will also be aimed at developing 'confidence'. Where has it been established that Scottish people lack confidence as a national group? The statement rounds off with the supposition that 'change' is required but change from what, to what, for what? Surely the aim to change something implies that what exists needs changing.

However, perhaps the more realistic expression to emerge from the Scottish Executive is the need for education to create *a work-ready, change-ready, learning workforce.*

Semantics and just semantics

A mark of thorough analysis is the effort to define one's terms. The above analysis of community education practices this to some extent. However, it tends to be a common response when looking at the words we use in professional practice for some to cry variations of the declaration 'that's all just semantics'. This is often a cloaked accusation that the person wanting to look at the meaning of an activity arising out of a title is in fact wasting everyone's time and being pedantic.

What we call something has an impact on how it is done. For example, a common aim for many youth workers is to 'make interventions'. It is a phrase deployed so often we have almost got to a stage that we use it apparently unconsciously or reflexively. But the word means 'interference' or 'incursion'. As such it represents an 'invasive' act. It is used in policing and medicine, but more tellingly in the military, where it is exposed for the euphemism it usually turns out to be; many recent violent (violating) actions in Afghanistan and Iraq have been called 'interventions'. We work with conscious, complex beings, so why would we not be careful of what our named strategies incline us to do? We might say 'oh that's not the same thing that I do' but until you analyse the action of 'intervention' how can you be so sure? And if what we do isn't 'intervention' in the way the army or the police might enact the notion, why do we continue to use the word? Is 'intervention' a common activity in youth work or is our skill more often attuned to allowing, making the space for, young people to approach us or be with us? Is it at least worth thinking about? Whatever, the notion and purpose of 'intervention' plays its part in ideologies of youth work and as such it is grist to the mill of analysis of the discipline. This is dealing with 'semantics' but it is not 'just semantics' because 'semantics' tend to direct and as such shape everything we do; 'intervention' and 'invitation' are not the same thing. Redundant words tend to go out of use. Subtle variations have an impact. If we set out on a journey together and you follow a compass bearing that is just half a degree different to the one I am following, after a days walk we are going to be miles apart.

The nature of this book

I have looked to make the material that follows accessible and digestible without patronising the reader. This being the case I have kept citation to a minimum, firstly because it interrupts the flow of what is an intentionally discursive style. I understand youth work to be more dialectical than dialogical in that in practice we tend to evoke ideas from ourselves and those we work with to create what is (for us and them) novel ways of seeing, understanding and interacting with the world; we do more than just 'chat'. As such, I have essentially presented discussions that are more dialectical than instructional. Secondly , this is not a formal or stereotypically academic book. I have generally used logical deconstruction of current paradigms, personal narrative, life story and metaphor as the means for the reader to begin to take a look at the fundamentals of our practice and question the 'taken-for-granted' notions that have at least become badly worn over the 40 or so years that many of them have been recycled in practice. That is a charitable response of course. In fact many of these sound bites that were never really relevant have become clearly redundant.

Adages like 'reflecting-in-and-on-action' and 'engaging in dialogue' are claimed as 'core skills' and are supposedly unique to our sector. I'm not sure the average youth worker does any better than my post-person, who is one of the finest listeners I've ever met. She often stands at the top of the street sorting her mail while young people, either going to school or on their lunch break, discuss issues with her as diverse as boyfriends and the Iraq war. The other day she whipped out a world map and was showing a group of 13 year olds (approximately) where Afghanistan is. They collectively worked out if it would be possible or indeed practical to drive there and back in a weekend! Political, social, formal, informal, community education? Does the label matter? The thing is they know her, like her and trust her. But they also know she has no official axe to grind and that she 'likes' them: she is not paid to seem as though she likes them and follow a particular organisational or state agenda.

At an instinctive level, humans are political beings. Our innate curiosity makes us that way. I don't think this postal worker is setting out to 'educate' anyone but she is involved in one or two of the most fulfilling of human pursuits, social interaction and dialectical discourse. And she is doing this with a group that engages in this with hunger, energy and enthusiasm: a section of the population that given the opportunity and appropriate circumstances will suck this kind of experience into their souls – young people.

On a number of occasions youth workers have told me that they see their learning about their practice as a 'ladder with no top'. I kind of know what they mean (I think) but a ladder with no top is not a ladder. A ladder with no top is something of a surrealist nightmare: a hell in which one would be obliged to climb, only certain that they were going nowhere while exerting effort to do so.

Such metaphors abound in our profession. However, they are made in the search for explanation and articulation rather than being consciously pretentious. Statements of this sort are encouraged by a latticework of irrational phrases or axioms of this type that proliferate within the youth work lexicon. They appear to have a profound meaning but are at best cryptic. We can call learning a 'ladder with no top' because we do not have a rational means to describe the nature of education and the purpose of professional training.

The provocation of thought and consideration

My own youth work training and education causes me to avoid 'shoulds' and 'musts' as they are largely not applicable (and other books addressing the field supply them aplenty). They are instructional words and I do not feel that much of my work is about instruction as I am chiefly concerned in my work with the honing of professional judgement that is more about folk reaching their own conclusions than following my (or others) instructions. Although this book is written with the authority of research, professional and academic discussion, practice experience and the use of logic (and does not proceed as a succession of questions) it is absolutely not a teaching manual – so please do not read it as such. That said, the commitment the work makes is to the provocation of thought and consideration as opposed to placing requirements on the reader to 'reflect' on or accept anything. What you do with it is your prerogative. That is a consequence of writing and the responsibility implicated in reading. But if you want a relatively inoffensive 'Highway Code' of youth work you can go to almost any website on the subject and get plenty of recipes, 'cook in the bag' options that either overtly or covertly claim to be 'the truth' or 'the way'. However, this book is looking more to engender dissent than recruit disciples. It will anger many of its readers. But it may also animate them and others.

Engendering dissent and effective professional judgement

I think we are obligated to develop a more political perspective on what we do. It is the lack of this that has done much to cause youth worker morale to plummet over the last two decades. Without a grasp on the nature of the social and political context of our work, we are obliged to merely adopt the purposes of employers, that are unavoidably driven by state ambitions and concerns. We become over burdened and under valued. This engenders frustration and to some extent confusion about our role. At that point we are left either with uncomfortable compliance, attempting to change the direction of society (a bit of a task for a full-time work force of a few tens of thousands whose record of industrial action has hardly sent the 'capitalist running dogs' into a panic) or plain personal defiance of our job descriptions – which ultimately is tantamount to professional suicide.

Comprehension of political purpose and critical engagement demonstrates the energising of *effective* professional judgement. This in turn produces authentically efficient practice and thus gives rise to job satisfaction, replacing role confusion with fulfilling and, at its best, joyful employment. The discussions below offer a path to this destination. Each might be read as 'stand-alone' positions, indeed this I believe is the best way to read the book; dipping in and out and perhaps re-reading parts after the whole has been digested. The connecting themes of the work are circumstances and ideas surrounding the delivery of practice, but these enduring strands are not a 'tramline narrative'. The issues looked at are eclectic and plucked from the wide range of questions and concerns that youth work might relate to. For all this, the themes do have logical connections and you will find a consistency of argument and critical engagement. However, I have worked with the contributors to this work to leave as much room as possible for the reader to make personal links to practice and to create their own associations between the elements that make up the whole. I hope this will mean that the work will be a different book for every individual that reads it; this would be in the best traditions of the making of professional judgement, creating the means for us to generate eclecticism rather than conformity and derive comprehension via diversity. The book is not looking to 'answer all the questions' but rather the topics covered have been chosen as areas ripe for review and as such useful means for the development of professional judgement.

Strengthening our professional position

Overall, although this is a critical work, it does not condemn any previous writing, other academics or thinkers. Most of the people I have met or had the honour to work with in any capacity involved in youth work were good, honest and diligent. Generally they labour, largely unappreciated, against tremendous odds to produce practice that has mostly left me in awe of the human spirit. But after writing close to 40 books, to a great extent avoiding the debates related to the field I have for more than half my life time been committed to and felt passionate about, I have produced something that I hope will strengthen our professional position.

I have throughout the text referred to 'we' and 'our'. I have done this because I continue to be a youth worker and feel I can quite rightly refer to myself as a member of that loose and turbulent fraternity. I have needed to reiterate several points in different ways, partly as some of these perspectives might be challenging and hard to ingest – they purposely counter traditions that many will hold dear – but also because I do not envisage or particularly recommend that this book is read in 'one hit' (from cover to cover) but rather used as an interrelated but semi-independent collection of discussions to be joined one or two at a time. As bedtime reading what follows is as likely to keep you awake as to lay you 'in the arms of Morpheus' but in the best youth work traditions, anything is worth a try.

Lastly, it is a common mistake in the investigation of social phenomena to present what is actually forecasting as logical outcomes. I'm unsure why writers have been drawn into this habit. Perhaps it is done in the hope that they can say 'I told you so!' This said getting involved with portents and omens incline us to overstate and embellish. As such I have sought to draw back from such prophetic indulgence. The demise of youth work has been predicted almost from the moment it emerged as a contemporary professional enterprise in the 1960s and continues up to the time of writing. However, reports of its death have been greatly exaggerated. Practice, because of it a diffuse and reoccurring nature, has proved very hard to extinguish. It's a bit like a forest fire; seemingly doused it sinks below the surface, but all it takes is a clear day, a bright sun and a strong breeze, and it's ablaze once again. This enduring quality indicates that youth work seems to be something post-World-War British society wants and needs. All it probably needs for its continuance is people ready to take part and do it. The raison d'être of the work I have done for most of my life, and by association this book, has been to this end.

References

Bryce, T.G.K and Humes, W.M. (2003) *Scottish Education*. Edinburgh University Press.
Descartes (2008) *Discourse on Method and the Meditations*. Penguin.

Acknowledgement

I'd like to thank all those who have contributed to the following pages, where appropriate names have been changed and locations generalised but I have reproduced people's responses as accurately as possible honouring their generosity and trust.

Education and Colonialisation

In this chapter I will present a number of the themes that re-emerge throughout the book. The chapter will start by looking at how young people might establish what they want and how this may not be via adult and professional interventions or incursions. I will go on, calling on Fanon, to discuss the conclusions and assumptions made about young people and draw attention to the analogous relationship between the coloniser and the colonised in the colonial context and that which exists between young people and adults and professionals in the contemporary era.

Other issues, such as education as a form of commodity, the difference between education, instruction, training and indoctrination will be touched on. The character and use of 'deficit models' will be introduced as will the idea that professional operations in the community context might be regarded more as the activity of state mediators rather than that of a relatively benign or neutral agency.

I was working in the Midlands a while ago and I got into a conversation with a research worker looking at the youth service. One of her findings was that only 35 per cent of those using the local youth provisions were female, for her this was 'disgraceful'. I asked her what she thought should be done about this. Her immediate answer was 'more activities in projects that appealed to young women, and less football and pool'. I asked, 'So football and pool don't appeal to young women?' She looked rather puzzled at this and asked if I felt football and pool appealed to young women. I said I was probably the wrong person to ask as I had just written an article about Jean Balukas (the former US Open Straight Pool Champion) while one of my great grandmothers had played for a good munitions football team during the First World War and had seen that experience as enriching and informing her life. She often said it made her see that women could 'do things for themselves and work with each other'.

I never found out what this person had in mind in terms of activities that might appeal to young women, but looking back on this short chat it seems to me that young women (or indeed, young men) will only begin to use youth facilities if and when they want to. If they do not, anything that she, or I, or you might do to 'make', persuade, or bribe them to use such facilities, needs to be enacted after asking a couple of questions; 'Why do we want to make young women (or young men) come to youth facilities anyway?' and 'What is it that is so 'worthwhile' about youth facilities?' It was during that same stay in the Midlands that a youth worker, Amanthi, told me:

Young people might learn things while being with youth workers, but they would learn things anyway even if there were no youth workers. Perhaps they would learn more if there were no youth workers, or they might learn more worthwhile things. Who can say with any surety? We set up situations where they might learn what our organisations want them to learn, but in my experience they sometimes learn very little about that stuff if anything and learn more about other things that no one could have predicted.

Where I work we got some funding for computer training. Quite a lot of resources really, including a number of computers and smart chairs and desks. We got a group of young women interested. Some came with a friend but most didn't know each other well at the outset. But they knew more collectively than the bloke who was hired to teach them. They taught him more than anything!

These young women became more of a social group and not so much a class. One person's mother's friend trained guide dogs and Jean came over to show the group a bit about how she trained them. They loved the dog of course, but the blind woman who she was training to use the dog had lost her sight while climbing in the Himalayas. None of the group had ever seen what you might call a mountain and they asked Rachael to came back to talk to the group about her experiences. She did, bringing a friend to work a powerpoint presentation (mostly pictures of climbing mountains) but during the course of this Rachel chatted about wanting to organise a group of blind kids from America to climb Snowdon. She had a connection with the American Foundation for the Blind (the AFB) I think. Each blind person needed a 'trek buddy', preferably of their own age. To cut a long story short the following year about half of what had started out as a 'computer training group' were climbing Snowdon with eight young blind American people.

I didn't really do anything to make that happen. I think what funding there was for it came from what Rachel raised, I think through the AFB and others, although we did arrange for the minibuses and worked with the group to book youth hostel places but they paid for that themselves. All I really had done was set up computer training that had been more or less useless to them.

Was the Snowdon thing education? No, it was more than education wasn't it. You don't 'learn' morality and empathy at that level. That is about higher consciousness and awareness. You 'live' that. But yes, if you sit down with a form you can tick off all sorts of things from it in terms of learning – but what does all that mean anyway? You get a pat on the head for jumbling a few ideas around to justify your own professional existence?

The thing that sticks in my mind most was one young woman telling me that the blind lad she was with, her 'trek buddy', was less scared than her on one of the really tricky parts. She froze. What Cherish had 'seen' was that her fear had its root in her ability to see. She saw, that at that moment, in that place, her sight had made her more 'disabled' (unable to do something) than her 'trek buddy'. Cherish said that 'six words Jim (her 'trek buddy') had said to her had got them across . . . 'Come on . . . We can do this'. Off the top of my head I might call that 'teamwork', 'working together for positive outcomes'. But for Cherish, it had been Jim who had got her over that ridge and not the other way round. That's more than education. That's epiphany! A sudden realization of the essence or meaning of our related condition.

Youth work is often about 'youth working' and not about working with or on youth. Youth 'works', if you know what I mean. It just 'works' because that's the nature of being young. That's how people grow up or mature with or without youth workers. The character of being young makes youth work. Youth workers are people that go along with this, people who don't stop it happening. We don't make it happen because no one can make it happen for someone else. Although I've known plenty of youth workers who seem to do their best to stop it happening. Not consciously in the main. I think by trying to make it happen.

A good thing for a youth worker to do is to do what they can to stop those who would maybe stop youth working from doing that. That's sometimes management committees or local authorities but it can also be parents, families, other young people and youth workers themselves. For a youth worker to do all that is quite hard work I think.

Currently it seems the social, economic and political environment, with some help from government policy, is more and more obliging young people to become involved with forms of quite formal youth work. This might just put more than 35 per cent of young women through the doors of the various agencies that are looking to recruit young people but that doesn't alter what seems to be an inescapable fact; the worst thing about youth facilities is that they are 'youth' facilities. As a youth, the last place I or anyone I knew wanted to go was a place designed for 'youth'. These 'sites' were places you were sent to by your parents, where you ended up if there was literally nowhere else to go. Either that, or somewhere I (like my peers) would pretend to be if I was actually going where my parents didn't want me to go. I know not everyone was or is like this, but perhaps around 65 per cent are (the approximate number of young people who don't attend youth provision).

How much room is there in our practice for people to make what there is what they want (as in the above example from Amanthi) if there are people employed to 'put on' what they, from their research, believe people want? One might well find that if one interviews 1,000 young women about what they want that those things will not be what the eight young women you are working with want. What they want might well grow out of their interaction rather than what they had originally perceived to be what they wanted. I don't think any of the young women attending the computer group above would have listed climbing Snowdon with American blind young people high on their 'wants list' before they turned up for the computer training.

Some wants and needs emerge from particular interactions rather than arrive ready formed in people's minds. Most of us, other than at a very superficial level, don't have much idea of what we want. Even if we do it's usually a surprisingly short list. Sometimes, even when we get what we thought we want, we conclude we never wanted it at all. The feeling that we wanted it was a mistake. We might have wanted the idea of 'it', but we didn't really want 'it'. For example, I wanted to play the saxophone. So I spent £300 on an instrument and found out where I could take lessons. But when it came to attending the lessons and undertaking the necessary practice, I realised, all things considered, that while I still wanted to play the saxophone, I didn't want it enough to do what was needed to achieve this end – I didn't *really* want to play the saxophone but I liked the idea of it. How often have any one of us walked a path like this? How often have I asked young people what they want and made as sure as I could they were making an 'informed choice', only to find out the only way to make an informed choice about doing something was to do it?

So we bought the decks, the weight training equipment, we raised funds for the street hockey kits . . . and pretty quickly stacked them away in the cupboards with all the other stuff people had at one time 'wanted'. And when we pulled it out a couple of times a year we'd be told 'this isn't the right stuff . . . you ought to get new stuff'.

Working on the basis of the stated 'wants' of a particular moment and place is not a fruitful pursuit; it is reacting to people as if all they stand for is what they can potentially consume. This gets to a point sometimes when we and they don't bother to differentiate between what might be a want and a need; we talk about people's 'wants and needs' as if they are the same things.

For most of the last quarter of the 20th century, a relatively small percentage of young people attended designated youth facilities for any significant part of their life before work. However, between the ages of 13 and 18, I didn't see myself as a 'youth' – that category, like 'adolescent', didn't mean a thing to me (and it still doesn't tell me much). Where did it come from? Who invented this label? Well, it was people like that researcher and it certainly wasn't 'youth' themselves. What is a 'young woman' anyway? Who decides which women are young? It would be interesting to go into a pub and ask all the young women to put their hands up, see what kind of response you get. Go into a school and ask for the same thing – I bet you that not all those you would categorise as 'young women' would identify themselves as such.

I went to a meeting on the first day of my second post as a professional youth worker after qualifying. I wanted to set up a group for young women as part of the new project I was hired to manage (although then as now I was not certain what a 'young woman' was – what about 'youngish' women?). I told the meeting that if anyone was interested or had any views on how this might be done that I'd be keen to talk to them. After the meeting the woman, who would many years later would become my wife, approached me and told me that she was speaking to me as a 'young woman'. I listened intently to her point of view. Unlike me she was local and had grown up in the area where I was going to work. In the course of our conversation I asked her how old she was. She told me she was 28. I didn't say as much at the time but to me, at 32, that wasn't very young and I certainly hadn't envisaged the young women's group serving 28 year olds.

A lot of people who you, I or that researcher might identify as 'young women' see themselves as 'girls' – a word that former *New Musical Express* and *The Face* writer Julie Burchill said brought to her mind 'a small, mobile unit' as opposed to the noun 'woman', a person 'tied to a womb'. But a 'girls night out' can involve women of almost any age. Others females see themselves as mature, old, middle-aged or just straight forward women or 'ladies'.

It seems drawing conclusions about people, what and who they are, what they might or might not want, where they should be or want to be, without much knowledge or understanding of them as individuals or groups is not very useful. Likewise plastering expectations and values on the make-up or 'participation profile' of youth facilities, looking to 'pump them up' to match particular cultural beliefs or political values, that might be quite alien to a particular locality or population, feels like an imposition.

The area of the Midlands where I met the researcher has been for decades very ethnically diverse, multiracial. It is made up of around 40 different cultural groups. Each group has unique traditions, but many traditions overlap in the working class melting pot. As such, there is a complexity of cultural, social, religious and class practices and conventions. To see the 'young women' from this melange of people as a kind of homogenous whole is the same kind of contorted perception the coloniser had of 'the native' in the 'days of Empire'. The 'natives' in lands colonised by Europeans were treated in a particular way, not like the colonisers treated each other. At the same time the colonisers wanted the 'natives' to act in ways that they (the colonisers) wanted; take on what the coloniser believed was 'good' for them, partake of the coloniser's religious practices, adopt the coloniser's value systems, enter the institutions (facilities) that the coloniser, in their benevolence and wisdom, prepared for the 'native' to 'benefit' from (churches, schools and yes even what we might recognise today as 'youth facilities').

It's not surprising that as a society, with the colonialisation era being historically a comparatively recent period, wherein most of our institutions (education, health, law etc.) were formed, we continue this culture of colonialisation. We are quite used to other people setting our social agenda. Many have become more or less passive with regard to our social expectations and as such we have evolved into relatively politically submissive beings – our wants are prescribed for us, by the paternalistic other, and we more or less accept this. Advertising and product placement are just the most obvious manifestations of this condition.

Take education. We, as a society, tend to agree that education is 'a good thing'. But is it? Why? How does education differ from wisdom? Is to be educated the same as being wise? In our society, at best, to be educated is to be steeped in some field of knowledge, felt to be of use to society; at worst it is associated with being 'skilled up' for employment. When I have knowledge of something that is of little use to society I'm not really thought of as educated. I may know everything there is to know about West Ham United, and as such I might be thought of as an expert on the good old Hammers, but this would not make me educated in the eyes of society. However, if I had a great deal of information about mathematics in my head (and for me that's a big if) most people would say that I was educated.

In our society education is a commodity. This is hardly surprising as we live in a capitalist society where most things and people are either commodities (things, skills or abilities to be sold) or consumers (people who buy commodities) and usually both. In general, the better educated I am (the more I have in terms of skills and useful knowledge that I can sell) the better I get on in society – in other words the more I adapt to this society the more advantages I have, although if I can buy stuff and sell it at a higher price than I paid for it (something which is astonishingly called 'fair trade') that will also provide me with financial advantages.

Although I may have my 'sellable knowledge' this does not mean that I am particularly wise, or aware. Education is not revelation nor is it the 'epiphany' experience had by Cherish on Snowdon. It is, for the vast majority of people, a form of indoctrination, a particular slant on information. As such, to be well educated in a consumerist society is to be well instructed or trained. Indeed, most folk would have trouble saying what the difference is between training and education – that's indoctrination for you! However we train (rather than educate) dogs and horses. Learning is always closely linked to education; someone might 'learn to drive' but this does not make them 'educated drivers'; we tend to have driving instructors rather than driving teachers.

While it might be true that many of us understand a lot of education to be a form of training (we have accepted this), to see training as education is to be indoctrinated. Why not call education 'training'? Well, education is not training – these are not just different words, they are different experiences, they have different uses and they do different things and have different effects on people. Training is essentially instructive; it is premised on a person or people developing skills and taking in/digesting firstly information and then, as their skills develop, knowledge. However, education essentially relies on questioning, argument or dissent. Education is the getting of knowledge via learning. Education might be thought of as a car travelling along the highway of learning between the hick town of Ignorance and the mighty metropolis of Knowledge. On the way there are petrol stations that offer five star questioning and Little Chefs that have a menu of argument and dissent. Intellectual activity, the means by which education happens, is by its very nature a sceptical pursuit, based on critique. You may need to apply intellect to training but to disagree with your trainer will risk causing them frustration, confusion and maybe anguish. This is because you have turned training into education (and they have only been paid to train you).

One may come to education with a basis of knowledge gained by instruction, just as a person who wants to become an artist might be able to draw and paint, but 'having knowledge' or a head full of 'facts' is not to be educated; the winner of 'Who Wants to be a Millionaire?' or 'The Weakest Link' is not necessarily the most educated of people. Indeed, the educated person might be so distracted asking themselves what they are doing appearing on 'The Weakest Link', or what the whole meaning of television game shows are, that they might not answer too many questions and become 'The Weakest Link'. . . Goodbye!

The public role of the educated intellectual is as an outsider, and disturber of the status quo. S/he is not an 'expert'; expertise is narrow knowledge. Using one's intellect, one's intelligence, leaves one with little alternative than to question received ideas and apparent understanding. According to Palestinian/American literary theorist and cultural critic Edward Said's *Representations of the Intellectual* (1994:x):

> One task of the intellectual is the effort to break down the stereotypes and reductive categories that limit human thought and communication.

Training, indoctrination and instruction mean that you learn 'the way': the way to drive; the way to eat your dinner, the way to 'do' informal education or 'supervise' someone. In turn, the ambition to get young women involved in informal education in a particular part of the Midlands, for example, is based on the assumption (hardly anyone has ever written to the council and demanded more informal education apart from a few unemployed informal educators perhaps) that they need informal education. But this is the working through of a deficit model of the type familiar within the colonial context. 'You, the native, need what I, the coloniser have. You have not asked me for it, indeed you avoid it, but one way or another, by reward or punishment, I will impart my notion of education, my religion, my values, my social norms to you, and, in the colonial situation, the better you take these on, the better you will fare'.

This system or process gives rise to the attitudes that the Martiniquais psychiatrist, philosopher, revolutionary and writer Franz Fanon observed in the Algerian colonial environment, what might be called 'the colonial mentality'. This is a kind of social pathology, wherein the colonised have habituated reliance on the coloniser. The goods of society are distributed according to the values and norms not of my culture, but of the colonising culture. I become a passive recipient of the favours given from what might be thought of as the active or controlling group (the former Black Panther Eldridge Cleaver (1971) also touched on this looking at the situation of young black men in the USA).

The colonised in such a society, according to Fanon display a number of typical traits; they are apathetic, both politically and socially, showing little interest in the overall solidarity of society. In competition for the limited resources that the coloniser makes available infighting between racial, tribal, family and other interest groups is constant. Ethnic or cultural boundaries become exaggerated in this rivalry (promoted and confirmed by the coloniser aided by the media which they own, direct and operate) differences are pronounced while commonalities between groups are understated.

These traits are evident in current British society, in particular among the young. It is hard to think of an era when the young have been so disaffected and many apparently lacking in life energy. From the earliest times the young have been a vibrant force in society (by its nature 'youth works', see Amanthi above). In the Middle Ages they were a major part of the workforce and had a voice. Medieval times saw great pilgrimages of children, petitioning the Pope and visiting holy shrines. In the 13th century there was a children's crusade (see Russell 1989, Raedts, 1977 and http://www.historyhouse.com/in_history/childrens_crusade/).

In the 19th and early 20th century they were involved in industrial conflict and school rebellions (see Higdon, 1984 and http://www.bbc.co.uk/radio4/history/longview/longview_20030408.shtml for example). Even as recent as the 1960s and 1970s students were involved in organised political action of the most dynamic and energetic sort (see 'When School Students Fought the System' – http://www.workersliberty.org/node/7058).

Now the relatively young, apart from the politically almost meaningless drink induced frenzies of violence on Friday and Saturday nights in high streets up and down the country, are the most passive of groups. Even when the government took away the very livelihood of students, the grant system, there was a kind of disgruntled murmur, a few grumbles and groans, but in the main this abuse was accepted without much of a fight. Alongside the seemingly long term aim of NVQing of the universe, the on-going increase in the cost of higher education equates to the dismantling of the sector as a means for the mass of people to habituate a questioning and critical outlook: there appears to be little in the way of social will to resist this.

Men and women, the young and old, black and white, Gay and straight, still however find time to fight and compete, with little sense of shared interest. Scotland, Wales and Northern Ireland are going their own way, London 'flicked the 'Vs' to everyone else ages ago, and we get a bonus Boris as a consolation prize. Like a toned down Yugoslavia in the latter days of that former country's existence, communities squabble and scramble in the competition for resources to plough their own particular furrow, premising their claims on contorted notions of justice or 'the good'. This keeps us involved in low level economic arguments about funding and the limited degree of control available outside the legitimate forms of social violence (that are in the hands of a quite independent army and a semi-autonomous police force).

The government encourages us to 'develop our communities' and 'community cohesion' which include some and exclude others, and with the aid of employed, community based professionals, these cohesive communities compete against each other for grants and government hand-outs on which their survival is dependent. This is the commoditisation of services and provision – 'all against all and the devil take the hindmost'. This is all encompassed under the commercially congruent label of 'social capital'.

This being the case, you can see that the society we live in is profoundly colonial.

The community-based professional (informal and community educators etc) is, in effect, an agent of this state; apparently all but disregarding the commonality of people's experience of exploitation while constantly reiterating ('celebrating') difference, emphasising 'cultural diversity' that plays a part in establishing the colonial ethic (deficit) at the local level.

The professional in the community in practice promotes competition for what resources there are by way of funding applications (so the best written applications win the dosh rather than the most deserving causes). At the same time the norms and values of elite and authority groups, framed in organisational aims and state policy, are passed on by the youth worker's use of informal education. As such, the youth worker, involved in 'community education' might be thought of as, what on 10 November 1963, in Detroit, USA, in his *Message to the Grass Roots* Malcolm X called, 'house niggers', trustees on the plantation (see http://www.american rhetoric.com/speeches/malcolmxgrassroots.htm).

In the colonial situation we are all as victims, both the colonised and the colonisers suffer – as Fanon points out, all are miserable in the colonial environment, no one is fully human.

What can we do? Well, there needs to be some reformulation of our role as professionals working in the community. Despite what some youth workers seem to think, we are not in a position to change the world; we find it hard enough to change our job descriptions! But we can look to initiate a reassessment of our personal/individual position; we can become, as Malcolm X might have put it, more like a 'field nigger'; someone who is supported by those we work with, rather than someone who comes in to do something to or with those people on the orders of 'the man'.

But if you are being paid as an employee of the state, the moment you show (rather than describe) yourself as an ally of those you work with, for and amongst, you risk being vilified, at best seen as a victim of the dreaded 'transference' ('going native') and at worst a malpractitioner. Try it. Abandon the badge of the informal educator and take up the torch of socialising knowledge and supporting the genuine politicisation of those you work with; you will soon, in one way or another be 'banged to rights' or so sidelined that it will seem that you are 'shouting at the rocks'. We need to be a bit smarter than this.

This analysis questions the professional role. I have examined and critiqued the situation of the professional in the community; you can agree or disagree, but it is likely that the journey will have helped you to see what you are, professionally, more clearly. It is only at this point that we can do anything at all about our situation . . . education, as Malcolm X might have it, 'by any means necessary'.

References

Burchill, J. www.julieburchill.org.uk
Cleaver, E. (1971) *Soul on Ice*. Panther.
Chief Secretary to Treasury (2003) *Every Child Matters*. TSO.

Fanon, F. (1967) *Black Skin, White Masks.* Grove Press.
Fanon, F. (1965) *The Wretched of the Earth.* MacGibbon and Kee.
Higdon, T.G. (1984) *The Burston Rebellion.* Trustees of the Burston Strike School.
Minister of Education for Scotland
http://www.bbc.co.uk/radio4/history/longview/longview20030408.shtml
Raedts, P. (1977) The Children's Crusade of 1212. *Journal of Medieval History*, 3.
Russell, F. (1984) Children's Crusade. In Strayer, J. *Dictionary of the Middle Ages.* Macmillan.
Said, E.W. (1994) *Representations of the Intellectual.* Vintage.
Sharma, S. and Gupta, A. (2005) *Tha Anthology of the State*. Wiley Blackwell.
When School Students Fought the System – http';//www.workersliberty.org/node/7058
http://www.americanrhetoric.com/speeches/malcolmxgrassroots.htm
X, Malcolm (1992) *By Any Means Necessary.* Pathfinder.

2

The State

In the previous chapter the association between the youth worker and the state was broached. In this chapter the notion of the state will be outlined in order that readers might better understand the character of the relationship that exists between the professional working in the community and the state, analysis of which will reoccur in subsequent chapters.

The following is not meant to be an exhaustive definition of the state but it might help orient those who are not familiar with using the concept in relation to practice, while providing a dialectical tool for those who might be practiced in relating to the professional/state alliance.

The state is generally thought of as the central concept in the study of politics. Probably a consequence of this is that its definition is the subject of passionate scholarly argument. In a political sense a state is a range of institutions that have the authority to make the rules, regulations and the laws which govern society. It also has internal and external sovereignty over a defined region or country. According to Louis Althusser institutions such as the church, trade unions and schools (implicating education in general) are part of an 'ideological state apparatus.' Youth work might be thought of as part of this ideological apparatus in that qualification to practice is sanctioned by the state and it is funded or resourced directly or indirectly by the state while its practice is shaped, defined, limited and directed by state legislation and policy (*Every Child Matters* etc.). This being the case the state can fund/resource a range of groups, organisations and institutions within society that, while being seemingly autonomous in principle, are in fact joined to and dependent upon state support, by way of finance, favour or other resources such as premises or land but importantly too, via law and policy.

For the seminal sociologist Max Weber the state is a system that has a 'monopoly on the legitimate use of physical force within a given territory.' As such, the state includes institutions like the courts, civil service, the armed forces and police. The state enforces its own legal order over its territory. Most Western states more or less comply with this definition.

The state, as a term, usually refers to all institutions of government or rule – modern and ancient. The modern state has a variety of traits that were originally established in the context of Western Europe, having their roots in the 15th century and culminating with the emergence of capitalism. It was in the 15th century that the term 'state' acquired its contemporary meaning. This being the case the word is often used when referring to the modern political system.

Broadly speaking a state, in international law, has:

- an enduring population
- a distinct territory
- government
- the means to enter into relations with the other states

Within a federal system, like the United States, 'state' also refers to political entities which are not totally independent, but subject to the authority of the wider federal union or state. The United Kingdom is a monarchical version of a federal state in that parts of it, Scotland, Northern Ireland and Wales, have different versions of the same institutions (parts of government and law for instance). Incidentally, the full title of the 'British Union' is 'The United Kingdom of Great Britain and Northern Ireland'.

In everyday parlance, the terms 'nation', 'country', and 'state' are often taken to mean the same thing, however a nation refers to a people who have origins, customs, and history in common while a country is a geographical area. The state is the governing institutions that have control over a specific territory. This territory can vary over time. British state influence 150 years ago took in its Empire and it was during the epoch of 'Imperial possession' that the main aspects of the British state were moulded into what they are today. Hence our society and its institutions, including education and welfare (so by association youth work) continues to be influenced by its colonial past.

The state is sometimes confused with government, but government is just one element of the state. The concept of government refers to the manner in which the highest political offices are awarded and the relationship that these offices have to each other and to the rest of society. The notion of government does not encompass other parts of the state. The 'state' is made up of the tools of political power, while government is the way in which these tools can be accessed and used. As such, the government while not being the state is a constituent part of the state, concerned with the formation and organisation of State control. The government can deploy other arms of the state, the armed forces and the police and services under state authority (even if mediated at a local level) health, education and social services, to deliver state discipline and exert control.

The phrase 'political system' is a sort of feeder concept to the notion of the state, referring to the plethora of social structures that work to generate the decisions that effectively bind society into a cultural and legal entity. In modern times, these would include the political regime, political parties, and various sorts of organisations.

Marxists argue that the formation of modern states can be explained primarily in terms of the interests and struggles of social classes. The state is controlled by an elite or ruling class. According to Miliband for instance the state is used by the ruling class as a means to oppress the rest of society via connections between state officials and economic elites. Miliband argues that the state is run by an elite group that share a common background with the capitalist class. This being the case, state officials have similar interests to the owners of capital and as such these groups are connected by a mass of political and interpersonal relations. In Britain's case this suggested relationship is made concrete by the relationship between the Crown and the state but more influentially the need to placate multinational corporate/capitalist interests to maintain private investment in British industry and commerce which has a crucial impact on employment and so tax income and the maintenance of services (including youth facilities and schools) those taxes fund. The British state also has to maintain a deep and profound association with global capitalist interests because of other complex issues such as its borrowing requirement, import and export agreements that are effectively 'managed' alongside other states' relations with dependency on the same nexus of global capitalist/multinational concerns. Recent events involving the Lockerbie Bombing, the British government and Libya demonstrate this nexus.

For all this, according to Michel Foucault political theory needs to detach itself from analysis of the state. For him, power in the contemporary world is diffused and decentralised, and is delivered by a much more varied array of instruments than was the case in the early modern era. As such, the idea of a centralised, controlling state is anachronistic. However, this outlook to some extent accommodates other theorists of the state who argue for a more detached or independent physics of state operation. This position has it that when capitalist states act on behalf of the ruling class it is not necessarily because of the deliberate endeavour of state officials, but rather it is a function of the 'structural' disposition of the state. That is, over time, the state has evolved to foster the interests and dominance of capital. This is a much more insidious perspective that understands the state and capital as associated entities quite independent of other considerations such as 'rights', 'democracy' and 'public opinion'. In fact, from this perspective, the state, allied to capital, shapes public opinion while framing laws and rights in order to support this associated interest. In this situation democracy is interpreted according to what is expedient for the maintenance and advancement of this alliance. As such the potential and limitations for social change and development is tightly controlled by particular and definite agenda.

Almost everyday we can perceive the 'movement' or activity of the state. For example, when there is talk about the 'privatisation of the National Health Service', the 'nationalisation of the railways', and the development of regulatory bodies we witness the precincts of the state shifting like tectonic plates.

However, suspicion and mystery have surrounded the 'quangos', quasi-autonomous organisations that appear to arise out of this process, many of which have proliferated in and on the periphery of the youth work sphere over the last decade. Their largely 'undemocratic' and interest related influence over practice and the delivery of state and government policy in part justifies the notion that the state operates independently of the will of the vast majority of the population.

The role and function of the state in our lives and the impact of corporate or capitalist activity on a global scale has given rise to a raft of critical literature over recent years. This, together with the rise of the internet, has made it increasingly more difficult for state and allied propaganda to camouflage the nature of what has been called the 'new world order'. The consequences of this have yet to be fully felt but perhaps the ubiquitous nature of both overt and covert surveillance and education, together with a higher level of professional incursions (interventions) particularly targeted on the most politically impressionable (the young) are part of the response.

Most critical theory relating to young people and education is applied to notions of schooling. This is sometimes used by youth workers as a 'get out of jail' card, as youth work as such is rarely not referred to. However, this is because youth work is for the most part simply overlooked by macro-educational theory as it is pretty much a backwater of the British educational and welfare systems. But this in fact does not free the profession from being morally implicated in the workings of the state and its institutions. As long as youth work associates itself with education it is caught in the web of state ambition in this field. This being the case in what follows I have taken referrals to 'schooling' as having a broad association with the education of young people, encompassing forms of so called informal education that youth workers see themselves delivering.

References

Barnes, J. (1999) *Capitalism's World Disorder*. New York: Pathfinder.

Carey, R. (Ed.) (2001) *The New Intifada*. London: Verso.

Chomsky, N. (1994) *World Orders, Old and New*. London: Pluto.

Chomsky, N. (1996) *Class Warfare*. London: Pluto.

Chomsky, N. (1999) *Profit Over People*. New York: Seven Stories.

Curtis, M. (1998) *The Great Deception*. London: Pluto.

Foucault, M. (2000) *Truth and Power in Power*. edited by Fearon, J.D. The New Press.

Hertz, N. (2001) *The Silent Takeover*. London: Heinemann.

Hoffer, E. (1951) *The True Believer*. New York: Harper Collins.

Klein, N. (2000) *No Logo*. London: Flamingo.

Miliband, R. (1983) *Class Power and State Power*: Verso.

Monbiot, G. (2003) *The Age of Consent*. Bury St Edmunds: Flamingo.

Moore, M. (2002) *Stupid White Men*. Harmondsworth: Penguin.

Palast, G. (2002) *The Best Democracy Money Can Buy*. London: Robinson.

Pilger, J. (1998) *Hidden Agendas*. London:Vintage.

Pilger, J. (2002) *The New Rules of the World*. London: Verso.

Pilger, J. (2003) *Web of Deceit*. London: Vintage.

Robson, J. (2001) *Them*. London: Picador.

Snow, N. (1998) *Propaganda Inc.* New York: Seven Stories.

Snow, N. (2003) *Information War*. New York: Seven Stories.

Weber, M. (1994) The Profession and Vocation of Politics. In *Political Writings*: Cambridge University Press.

3

The Question of Change

Over the past 20 or so years, a perennial consideration for managers in the education and welfare fields has been the notion of 'change'. At the same time the word or ambition to enact change has been a central feature of much of the theory and policy surrounding youth work. It has been wheeled out as the need to 'manage', 'confront' or 'cope with change'. In the last few years it has become a sort of 'war cry' of the methodology of informal and community education within the youth work sphere; a 'commitment to change' has become a primary aim for young people, though at times it is not clear change from what, to what and why. The Tom Peters' idiom of 'Thriving on Chaos' (1989) made a lot of money for big Tom, while others wrote, and still write, best sellers on 'initiating', 'predicting' or 'understanding' change. Change has become like a physical thing; a dragon or an elephant that either is there or not. It apparently needs to be caged, trained or processed. Sometimes it 'happens' and sometimes it doesn't. Whatever the case, youth workers, and the language of informal education eulogises change as a sort of overarching priority for people and communities.

In this chapter I will look at the nature of change and assess what might be meant by 'change'. I will deconstruct the usage of the idea of change in the youth work realm in order to help practitioners critically analyse the place and purpose of 'initiating change' within professional practice.

The purpose for and place of 'initiating change' in contemporary youth work practice is quite remarkable given that 'change' is an unavoidable consequence of living within time. I am not the first to notice this. The Greek philosopher Heraclitus in around 400 BC proclaimed that, 'All is flux, nothing is stationary'. Sceptics like Alphonse Karr in the first part of the 20th century, argued that 'the more things change, the more they are the same'. He may have felt confirmed by the many reorganisations of local government, the youth service, education and the health service that we have seen over the last 40 years, and there is something to what he was saying. But analysing change seems futile as change is largely reliant on perception and takes place via time that brings with it (inevitably) change.

Dealing with change

It seems clear that we can't choose not to deal with change; we kind of have to deal with it. Some might say that they, or people they know, deal better or worse with change than others. But how is this? Do they have a genetic propensity for it? Or is it that they have a social advantage of some sort? How do you measure how well someone has done in terms of changing? Are some individuals good at all types of change; sex, dance steps, food? Are others at an advantage in specific areas? I am good at dealing with a change of house, but bad at coping with a change of partner. What is change? Is moving my desk change? If it is I'm good at that.

It is not uncommon to hear people make declarations like, 'She just refused to change' or 'He is stuck in the past', but such propositions are nonsense. One cannot refuse to change and we all live quite definitely in the present. After all, as the Rev. John Haynes Holmes had it, in *A Sensible Man's View of Religion* (1932) 'The universe is not a hostile, nor a friendly place. It is indifferent. Change isn't something we choose to be part of or not; it just is'.

Edmund Spenser, in the 16th century, argued in *The Fairie Queen*:

What man that sees the ever-whirling wheel
Of change, the which all mortal things doth sway
But that thereby doth find, and plainly feel
How Mutability in them doth play
Her cruel sports, to many men's decay?

And according to Shelley in *Mutability* 'Naught may endure but mutability . . .'

However, observations of this type seem more or less to have been ignored given the massive attention given to instigating, managing and 'innovating' change (making original changes!).Would it be more helpful to think about adaptability? But adapt to what if not change? If we say that someone copes well with change, we are not talking about the change itself, we are making a statement about a person's ability to deal with, cope within, meet or manage change. From this perspective we have a kind of Darwinian prospect. The lesser-spotted client adapts best to change so it is less likely to become extinct. Change is adaptation, success is survival. The client is basically reactive and passive in terms of change, not being an agent of change. Just someone that adapts to it. Are some people more in charge of change than others, as suggested by the millions of words written about 'making change happen'? It appears to be something we can be trained to do. This implies that if we don't make change happen things will stay the same. I put this to someone hosting a seminar on change and she told me that 'making change happen wasn't a statement about general change; it was a suggestion that we can make changes to certain situations or in particular instances.' This is a contention that we can change the specific but not the global. However, as soon as you make a change at the atomic level you have made a change that potentially has universal effects. The nature of change is that a change in one thing triggers a change in other things around it. A person double-parks in Islington to go into a shop and the traffic is gridlocked in Holloway; one aircraft is forced to drop altitude by 500 feet and all the aircraft around it are obliged to alter their flight paths. The cancer that kills starts at a molecular level.

The fact that slight change drives general change is confirmed by Werner Heisenberg's 'Uncertainty Principle'. In 1927 Heisenberg had it (how do these conversations start?) that at the subatomic level the only way to measure a system is to interfere with that system. That is, to observe a particle, you need to bounce another particle off of it which affects the motion of the particle being observed, which makes it measurable. So, if one wants to measure say the position of an electron, the speed of that electron must inevitably be affected. The particle used to make the observation of the position of the electron has affected the speed of the electron. This being the case, the very act of observation changes the system. We can be sure of the speed or the position but not both. This demonstrates that observation is itself an act that has effects. The effects of tree falling down in a forest unobserved are potentially different if I observe the tree falling down by the very fact that as an event it now exists in my memory; I can report it, write a poem about it, identify reasons for it and perhaps prevent other trees (that might otherwise have fallen down) from falling down by extrapolating evidence from my observations for this purpose.

The above indicates that there is no such thing as particular or general change. Change is an 'inclusive' process; it spreads like ripples in a pond except that rather than the ripples becoming necessarily less turbulent as they expand, the ripples of change can dissipate or create greater volatility as they effect all around them.

In youth work, when we talk about communities, individuals and groups 'needing to change'. There are various predicates to change, 'effective change', 'commitment to change' and 'initiating change'. But who is it that does the initiating (or the committing)? Who judges what is 'effective' or 'committed' and by what criteria? What changes are we talking about? Presumably we are not referring to climate. We refer to clients or whole communities 'needing to change'. However, the change the client is seen to need to deal with may be organisational, that is it has an origin in human activity and not the relatively mysterious foibles of the weather or an act of God, for example. We can't use the Darwinian model because it is not really a case of the evolving client, who, by stages of adaptation, comes to acclimatise or die. Statements like he 'changed direction' or she 'changed her outlook/perspective' appear to be putting forward the idea that the 'change' youth work is concerned with is chiefly psychological. Taking this to its logical conclusion it suggests that contexts (community settings, for example) are at best secondary. The fact that I might be in prison is not the real problem, my difficulties stem from the way I think about myself in prison and/or how I perceive prison. This feels like the last paragraph of every self-help book on the library shelf. In practice it asks me to believe that by 're-framing' my position, my position changes; if I can only get my head round that one I'll be OK (and you'll be OK – perhaps most of all Tom Harris will be OK, or he would be if he hadn't have died in 1995). But isn't this, albeit a nice idea, a lie? I can pretend I'm not starving, but that doesn't mean I won't starve to death. I can kid myself that the pain in my head is a demon or my imagination, but it will still be the tumour that kills me. I might convince myself I'm Napoleon, but I might not be victorious at Austerlitz.

The thinking that we can 'control' change (make it happen or be more or less committed to it) goes back a long way. Aztecs made human sacrifices to placate their gods (mostly in terms of the weather – Peter Cockcroft eat your heart out . . . literally) and how many goats have died for 'the gods'? Confucius had it that; 'They must often change who would be constant in happiness or wisdom'. Here 'Master Kong' seems to be suggesting that we can and should 'activate' change; we are being told that if we are to be happy and/or wise we must not only live and adapt to change, but seek to make changes. Karl Marx seemed to go along with this in his insistence that, 'The philosophers have only interpreted the world in various ways: the point is to change it.' But do we just change things for the sake of it? Some people believe in this. Indeed, the 'if it ain't broke why mend it' school does not have many adherents these days. This is understandable. If humankind had taken this attitude there would have been little reason, apart from necessity, to come down from the trees (apologies to creationists who, according to them anyway, have yet to evolve at all). What we know of the evolution of homo sapiens necessity has not been a consistently driving force; it has been punctuated by curiosity and adventurousness.

The mere 'commitment to change' does not ensure any benefits, indeed it can be a disastrous faith (commitment being a corollary of faith). Under the regime of Martin Winter, who became the first elected Mayor of Doncaster in 2002 (democracy, as the youth work canon tells us, is practically always a good thing) a great deal of change has occurred in that area. Over the recent past a huge amount of money has been spent on sprawling and ambitious commercial building projects. But these grand, ultramodern, monuments to change, some with waterside, park-like settings, have largely remained empty and unused while public housing has continued its long decline.

The consequence of the cost of this change has been cuts in services, not least Doncaster's early years and child care services, which four years after Council officials were warned that their actions were putting children's lives at risk, Ofsted (in 2008) identified as being among the worst in the country. A sad example of this was Amy, who two days before Christmas in 2007 was murdered by her father, who snapped his 16 month old daughter's spine. Amy was found to have been malnourished, dehydrated and had numerous fractures to her arms and legs. A few months later in another part of Doncaster, Alfie Goddard was squeezed, shaken, and thrown down the stairs of his home by his father. He was three months old when he died. Amy and Alfie are two of seven children who have been the subject of serious case reviews in Doncaster since 2004. Serious case reviews, or SCRs, are multi-agency investigations carried out when abuse, neglect, or a failure by child protection agencies are known or suspected to have played a part in death. The children include Cameron McWilliams, a 10-year-old who hanged himself, and Warren Jobling, a disabled boy who was in respite care at the time of his death. Warren's parents are suing Doncaster Council for, they say, failing to adequately monitor their son's carer. Only three of the serious case reviews have been published to date. They include a baby, known as 'Child A', who died in the same month as Amy.

It seems that while promoting 'commitment to change' in the community context we might need to be wary of possible 'over commitment to change'. There is change that can be seen from miles away, like great and grand buildings, and as such be tangible celebrations that change has been achieved, but it seems that 'hidden' changes that have every chance of remaining unseen can be insidious. It is possible that we in fact have no idea of how many children have suffered and maybe died in Doncaster since Mayor Winter 'committed to change'.

Often, things that look like major change are not, and things that intend to create drastic changes do not, in themselves, change very much. They seem designed merely to propagate the existing culture. But it is too much to say that 'things become the same'. If things stay the same, which nothing does, then it is not becoming anything; it is staying the same thing – which as we have seen, is paradoxical in terms of the logic of change. I think we have established that change is unavoidable, but how can we say that it is, a priori, positive, as Confucius, Marx or *Every Child Matters* might have us believe. How does change make us wise or 'happy'? Edmund Burke said that, 'a state without the means of change is without the means of its conservation'. This takes us back to Darwin, or forward if you were Burke, who was saying that we have to change if we are to carry on; like if we don't change we will be the very opposite to happy and wise, we will be stupid and dead. John Stuart Mill, a contemporary of Darwin, would have had no argument with Burke on this point, but he gives us a more expansive conclusion. For him, 'No great improvements in the lot of mankind are possible until a great change takes place in the fundamental constitution of their modes of thought'. The American author and philosopher Henry Thoreau had a similar hypothesis insisting that 'Things do not change; we change'.

You see, change is not something we are more or less good at, but the practice of perception is something that differs from person to person. My reaction to change is premised on my ability to perceive change. I can't believe the statement 'things never change around here' because it is actually completely unbelievable (paradoxical). But if you are blind to change (or your mind just won't accept the impossibility of things staying the same) you can't react to it. If one is unable to act on change it is unlikely that one will be able to initiate change; you will just be a slave to events. Likewise, the person who complains that everything is always changing is also not seeing the trees for the wood. They have in their head an ideal of a moment or time of non-change. They might call it 'consolidation' or 'reconciliation', but their fantasy is that there might be fallow periods in the process of time; this (as we have seen) is an illusion.

In *Of Human Bondage* (1920) Somerset Maugham described one of his characters as being 'like all weak men' as he 'laid an exaggerated stress on not changing one's mind'.

In his book *Education for Liberation* (1973) Adam Curle argues that, 'Education enslaves: men and women become free through their own efforts. He went on to say that his discovery of what he called '. . . this harsh fact . . .' challenged the work he had spent half his life doing. He came to this conclusion through his experience in and observation of education – the 'failures and miseries and . . . the occasional shafts of light'. He changed his mind about education.

It is this 'change of mind' that is so important in youth work and related disciplines. The wish for 'sameness' is damaging because it is unrealistic; it condemns us to disappointment, confusion and maybe worse as things continue to change. A great deal of emphasis is placed on decision-making in youth work (on the part of young people, community and professionals), but having made the decision the urban myth is that we should stick with that decision. This limits any decision making process, restricting us to just one decision. It means, in other words, the unimaginative will inherit the earth.

Creativity comes out of the changing of minds, as minds change perceptions alter and so do things. I might not be able to change the fact that I am in prison and thinking about prison in a 'different way' will not alter my state of incarceration. But I can do things with being in prison; I might not be able to change prison, but prison can change me. The stagnant, unchanging mind that lives in the dream world where change is optional will not be happy, it will not be wise and, in the end, will perish. Change, as a notion, an idea, a concept, is related to time which of course is mediated by our mind and as such our attitude to it is governed by our perception. We see the world and we see it changing; this is not necessarily 'how it is', but it is how we see it.

Our ability to 'come to terms' with change can only be by dealing with emotions and feelings that are interior. Change is not only something that happens to us, we happen and we denote change. If you like, change happens as part of our very being. In effect when we talk of coping with change, we are talking about controlling ourselves and the way we look at and experience the world. The prison is the prison and change, like time, cannot be managed. But we can manage ourselves (management being logical intentions rationally enacted) within the prison and within time, and we can only manage ourselves in the flow of change (we are not in charge of change but we can be in charge of ourselves in change).

Thus our ambitions need to be more focused, but not on the demons of time, the dragons of change, but on the spirit that is 'us'; where we are, in prison, in time and in change. Our actions in the ocean of change may speed up or slow down change, but this is a miniscule difference in the eternity that is the journey of change. We exist in change, we are of change, we are constructs of change and seeing this, even celebrating it, enables us to 'ride' change in a way that denying change or thinking we can control change itself does not allow. Hence one of the important pillars of youth work education is recognising change, its possible consequences, readying ourselves for these and finding ways to take advantage of changes in the cause of those we work for and amongst. In our work context, the community, we become effective by being sensitive to change and therefore be in a position to manage ourselves in that flow. This is not planning (which is a structured illusion that we can foretell the future and control it). It is preparation;

the laying out of options, given what we know and can reasonably conject – a constantly changing construct that prioritises sensitivity to change (we build in flux dampers!). The changes we make are in response to greater change but they, at a molecular level, are part of the change, which in terms of our personal experience can change the nature of change – all change changes things. So while a change might not be as good as a rest, a rest might be a nice change. In other words everything is change: we are in it, and of it. Understanding this part of knowing who and what we are.

References

Burke, E. (2006) *Reflections on the Revolution in France.* Dover Publications.

Curle, A. (1973) *Education for Liberation.* Tavistock Publications.

Harris, T.A. (1969) *I'm OK, You're OK.* Harper.

Haynes, H.J. (1932) The Sensible Man's View Of Religion. *The Community Pulpit.*

Heisenberg, W. (1990) *Physics and Philosophy: The Revolution in Modern Science.* Penguin. www.aip.org/history/heisenber

Kahn, C.H. (Ed.) (2008) *The Art and Thought of Heraclitus: A New Arrangement and Translation of the Fragments with Literary and Philosophical Commentary.* Cambridge University Press.

Karr, A. (1856) *A Tour Round My Garden.* Routledge.

Marx, K. and Engles, F. (1888) *The Communist Manifesto.* Houghton Mifflin.

Peters, T. (1989) *Thriving on Chaos: Handbook for a Management Revolution.* Harper Perennial.

Salmon, W.C. (Ed.) (2001) *Zeno's Paradoxes.* Hackett Publishing.

Shelly, P.B. (1997) *The Complete Poems of Shelley.* Random House. www.netpoets.com/classic/poems/057013

Sia, A. (1997) *The Complete Analects of Confucius.* Asiapac Books.

Smith, G.W. (1998) *John Stuart Mill's Social and Political Thought.* Routledge.

Somerset Maugham, W. (2000) *Of Human Bondage.* Vintage.

Spenser, E. (1853) *The Faerie Queene.* Routledge.

Thoreau, H.D. (2008) *The Writings of Henry David Thoreau.* BiblioBazaar.

4

Change, Compliance and Colonisation

On the basis of the analysis developed in the previous chapter the following will explore the use of the idea of change in the promotion of compliance via state/professional alliance. I will look at the ambition to change as a potential assault on targeted cultures and question the ethics of such practice. At the same time the potential of the profession to initiate change will questioned. Calling on Illich the chapter will go on to examine how the 'change agenda' can be deployed to promote deficit models of practice. Using Fanon I will demonstrate how this might perpetuate a 'colonial mentality'. I will use Guevara to offer an alternative perspective on change that focuses primarily on the professional as the subject of change.

I first heard the Drummers of Burundi when I was a 'Sniper', one of West Ham United's young army of followers, the junior version of the 'Mile End Mob' that was to evolve into 'The Inter-City Firm' celebrated in the books of Cass Pennant. It was on the juke box at the Custom House Workingman's Club, deep in the darkest Docklands of East London. It was an odd place to find such music. I was about 13. Straight away I loved it. It went directly into my soul and expressed all the defiance, rebellion and anguish I felt at that time. It confirmed something but at the same time changed things for me in that confirmation. I perceived that someone was thinking like me; someone felt what I felt because I felt the affinity (although I have never met a Burundi drummer to affirm this feeling).

Since then I have taken an interest in the Burundi Drummers and have found that no 'people professionals' helped them play their tunes, no one sought to 'change' them or me (up to that time) in some 'cultural project'. What they had, what they gave and still give to me, is something deeply bound up with identity, tradition and place. In short, that music is an expression of who they are and has not been planted or transplanted from somewhere else. Or that is what I perceive to be the case.

Michel Foucault, notably in his work *Discipline and Punish* (1977) has demonstrated how social interventions, carried out by the agencies of the state or organisations allied to the state through funding, whose aims and ambitions are often mediated by professionals, are premised in the need society has to control and create social conformity – to produce a compliant society and promote particular types of cultural norms that do not threaten or question the given social status quo. The professional operating in the social sphere is part of and defined by this activity. The state, either directly or indirectly, will not tolerate or fund activity that is contrary to its values or which fail to confirm its basis that is the inequalities inherent to any capitalist system.

From this perspective, the professional youth worker's ambition to 'change' could be seen as colonising activity wherein 'the client' becomes the object of 'cultural assault'. The professional comes along with their 'cultural armoury' and sets about transplanting their cultural understanding, the product of the state-funded professional training programmes, in areas, districts and communities that have their own cultural expressions. The agencies that employ professionals do not recognise, value or approve of these cultures and find them threatening, maybe because they are classed as criminal or deviant (that is why they perceive that they need changing) a bit like how the kind of musical expression the Burundi Drummers transmit might have been received by the first colonists that came across such 'sounds'. Whatever the case, the youth worker's brief is to initiate 'change' in the 'targeted' group. In harsh times the promise of simple change is seductive. The election of Barak Obama in the USA and the Japanese Democratic Party in August 2009, both successes were premised on the straightforward commitment to change, however, the proposal that the professional might be charged with changing others is ethically questionable, but the problem is often circumvented in professional aims by framing change *within the process of working with individuals to make change possible*? While there seems to be an inherent proposition in this instruction that at least part of what the professional might be involved with is acclimatising, mentoring or building 'factories for' change, the task appears to be asking for the generation of a situation that can be used (but not necessarily) by people to change rather than declaring that it is specifically the professionals' role to change people.

This might be making a trivial distinction, as while the focus appears to concentrate on providing a situation which may (or may not) be used for changing, the professional, by creating an environment primed for alteration, installing the 'apparatus' of the 'system' or 'academy' for change', would, as such, be the potential (and probably actual) 'agent of change' (or at least part of the creation of 'change ready' workforce). Thus, would it not be unrealistic to expect that a person not essentially looking to change to enter an environment that 'fosters' change, specifically calculated to smooth the progress of change, inhabited by professionals trained ('skilled up for') and inclined to initiate conversations and relationships geared to coax, coach or create hot-houses of alteration, geared to getting folk to 'commit to change', would not be influenced by the general psychosomatic matrix of change, the maelstrom of modification? How could anyone be definitely immune from being included in the overall psychological programme of this 'change factory'?

This whole scenario might be no more than academic: change, as we have seen, occurs constantly, no matter what we do or don't do. Also an individual may be as provoked, motivated or goaded to take a certain path by the insistence of someone else that they shouldn't follow a certain direction as they would by someone looking to 'facilitate' them in taking that same route. It is maybe somewhat naïve to take too lightly the power of defiance and the drive that some of us have to mutiny against 'good advice' and/or the manipulation of others?

Some people are quite good at looking as if they have changed or are changing when they are not (and vice versa). This is sometimes a low level survival mechanism. At the same time individuals can and do learn to make others in authority believe that they are thinking what the influential person wants them to think (see Erving Goffman, *The Presentation of Self in Everyday Life*).

The action of the change agent is not restricted to one potential outcome; it is often taken for granted that a youth worker acting to evoke positive change will do just that. As can be seen below, logically speaking there is as much chance of no reaction or 'negative change' as there is 'positive change'. At the same time there is little in the way of sturdy evidence that this situation would be any different if there were no change agent activity (illustrated opposite).

Are we really able to change another person if change is reliant on the will and action of the person changing? One might be able to change the actions of another person by bribery, persuasion or force and it is debatable if professional activity is not capable of at least two of these three options. For all this, if we are incapable of changing others how can we claim (as we often do) that we can make them 'comfortable', 'think' or 'educate' them?

Planning for change

This is something that has come to be a bit of a mantra in work with young people. But if one makes a plan for change for someone else and that plan is successful, what has actually happened is conforming to that plan (not change derived from that plan). This aside, successfully planned change is usually, by necessity, very limited in nature and probably set over quite a restricted time frame as the variables involved in long term, complex change would probably be impossible to predict. Change is built on the foundations of continuity; we can only move from one place to another from where we are at any point in time.

The longer the move the more unpredictable our final destination will be. The NASA space programme was built on the premise of making relatively tiny but incredibly numerous steps rather than giant leaps; progress was based on moving off from comparatively sure ground. So rather than seeing a mission making the jump from earth to moon, succession was marked out in change achieved from minute to minute and even second to second. This meant that a level of 'improvisation' was involved, allowing for small, often innovative, adjustments, possibly enacted at very short intervals, to pull missions back on track if they strayed due to unforeseen occurrences or conditions. To this extent every individual mission (and potentially every moment of each mission) was a learning and relearning situation wherein nothing was taken for granted (not even the overall plan of the mission). This is why very experienced pilots were used; people well versed in using their 'professional judgement' in what were more or less

Intervention	Possible responses to intervention	Outcome
Professional facilitates 'positive change'	Client is motivated to change positively'	Positive change'
Professional facilitates 'positive change'	Client attempts to take advantage of facilitation of 'positive change' but fails	No change or 'Negative change' or 'Positive change' (caused/motivated by something else)
Professional facilitates 'positive change'	Client ignores facilitation of 'positive change'	No change or 'Negative change' or 'Positive change' (caused/motivated by something else)
Professional facilitates 'positive 'change	Client is provoked to defy facilitation of 'positive change' and stays the same	No change or 'Negative change' or 'Positive change' (caused/motivated by something else)
Professional facilitates 'positive change'	Client is provoked to defy facilitation of 'positive change' and adopts 'negative change'	Negative change
Professional does not make any conscious effort to facilitate change	Client changes positively'	Positive change'
Professional does not make any conscious effort to facilitate change	Client attempts to 'positively change' but fails	No change or 'Negative change' or 'Positive change' (caused/motivated by something else)
Professional does not make any conscious effort to facilitate change	Client does not change	No change or 'Negative change' or 'Positive change' (caused/motivated by something else)
Professional does not make any conscious effort to facilitate change	Client 'changes negatively'	'Negative change'

unpredictable situations. With this in mind it is interesting that work with young people is often referred to as being characterised by unpredictability.

In terms of providing opportunities for 'change' and 'commitment' to the same it might useful for the professional to ask why our potential role as 'provocateurs' in the 'transmutation' of others seems to have become quite central to our practice in terms of organisational direction and policy. This does not appear to be about change for change sake or personal change on the level say like becoming a vegetarian or giving up Methodism to become a Baptist. Looking at the general focus on 'youth change' it is apparently linked with state initiatives around social issues like sexual activity, employment and crime. Sets of assumptions (in practice policy, government rhetoric and the media) exist which imply, or plainly state, that particular problematic youth groups and individual young people need to be 'open' and 'committed' to 'change'. In practice this translates as the requirement of young people to adopt less problematic profiles or to conform to particular general external standards.

The limits to change

Ivan Illich, particularly in *The Limits to Medicine* (1976) has pointed out that forms of professional intervention are ultimately damaging to those 'targeted'. He calls this (in the context of health) the *Political transmission of Iatrogenic disease.* The process starts by someone being seen to have a 'lack' that can be interpreted as pathological. I would suggest that this 'deficit model' is quite pervasive in terms of the professional focus. For example, the wish, desire or agenda to 'change' presupposes that a group are in need of 'change'; something about them needs altering, their behaviour in particular is seen as beyond the 'cultural pale'. The excuse to introduce the change is set up by the portrayal of the targeted group as lacking elemental input, such as education or socialisation or they are assumed to have a psychological deficiency (even though relatively few youth workers are qualified psychologists/psychiatrists). For instance, the prognosis of 'poor self-esteem' is made as if the professional was dealing with an endemic condition or disease and that the appropriate treatment is to 'change' the 'infected' person (expressions referring to 'betterment', ambitions to 'make them better' are openly used) to bring them into line with acceptable norms of behaviour. The state aims for this are called 'effective change' in the professional realm and this is achieved by the client's movement towards 'commitment to change'. When attempts to change behaviour do not work it is said that the attempts to achieve change were not effective and other forces can be let loose (young offender's teams, the police etc).

But the more or less effective 'treatment' (what has become known as 'intervention' in youth work) devalues the existing cultural expressions and products of that person (or community) and ultimately undermines the cultural cement that binds particular communities together. For example, I can convince, persuade, cajole or bribe a person to stop swearing although swearing is very much part of their life. It can have a positively beautiful, almost guttural poetry about it, which almost speaks as though the whole body is expressing itself out of impulse in reaction to something, rather than pondering some cleverly-thought-out phrase that can turn a response to bland cleverness. Everyone who ever loved or cared for them swears; all their friends swear; the mother at whose breast they fed swears; the uncle who came to visit them in hospital, the aunt who paid their bail – both swear. But I, the youth worker, seeking to make this person 'better', in one way or another, questions whether this swearing is something they, for their own good, might (should) change (swearing is after all 'wrong'). It doesn't take much imagination to understand the possible repercussions for this young person seeking to 'fit-in' to their community. At this point cultural colonialism can be seen to have taken place (*Iatrogenesis* – being made sick by treatment).

As pointed out previously, Franz Fanon (who was a qualified and experienced psychiatrist) in his books *Black Skin, White Masks* (1967) and *The Wretched of the Earth* (1965) pointed out the effects of this process in the colonial realm, creating what might be thought of as a *colonial mentality*. At its worst those colonised see themselves, their 'native identity', has having little if any value. Self- and group-worth are estimated on the level of approval that the coloniser gives. This approval is based on how close 'the native' has come to replicating the mannerisms, ways and cultural mores of the coloniser; black skins, white masks. However, it is always recognised that the approved actions are merely replicas and not 'the real thing'. Hence the very soul of the colonised is exterminated – they thus become the 'wretched of the earth'. How often, albeit entirely unintentionally, is the professional youth worker in fact an agent of this type of colonialism?

Given all of this, I feel that we might recognise that the emphasis, the language of 'change', and the very ambition to change others, has underlying values of a particular colonial/control milieu and social orientations attached. Why do we seek to 'change'? Why do we see that people, by their very essence, through their innate social interactivity, are in need of us bringing them 'opportunities to change'? As argued in the previous chapter, change happens continuously, without the intervention of professionals: 'agents of change' are only needed when the change required is something specific to the needs of a particular interest group that wants another group changed.

I suspect those we seek to 'change', those who by dint we see as (even if we don't call them) the 'abnormal' (the change usually has a 'normalising' function, referring to criminality, sexual behaviour, health etc.). The wretched of the earth are thus labelled because their cultural activities and/or values challenge or even intimidate other personal or cultural sensibilities, which of course are the product of particular class and cultural realms. This is why they must change, but not just change; the change that is required is one that will bring those changing closer to how those who employ agents of change, for whatever reason, want them to be.

This change can be like throwing sweets into a crowd. People will pick them up, eat them; they're free, taste nice and can help bring people together; something to share, enjoy. But this doesn't mean sweets are good for them. They rot your teeth, are full of questionable chemicals and make you fat. Maybe they raise your blood sugar and make you tired but fidgety. They might affect your concentration levels, making your thought processes less able to function and spoil your appetite for the good, if relatively bland, food that awaits you at home (*Iatrogenesis*).

What I would like to think is, if I enter a community, I will first look to be changed by and thorough that community's cultural expressions rather than, in the first instance, seek to promote the ideas I might import into that community. Che Guevara in his *Guerrilla Warfare* (1961) tells us that it is not possible for the Guerrilla to support or define the community. For the Guerrilla to be successful they must be ready to be defined (changed) by the community and look to be supported by them. This is the reverse, the antithesis of the deficit model, but it is not easy and maybe impossible for us to sustain. Cultural expressions involving what society might see as forms of vandalism, crime, drug abuse, copious consumption of alcohol, hooliganism, particular sexual practices, language forms that we might find abusive or even violent may need to be embraced rather than merely tolerated (toleration is a form of patronage and as such related to forms of deficit thinking).

If I can learn to welcome the storm, find its human and humane root and essence I might be able, by my participation in that culture, and having developed my own cultural horizons, to become a contributor to the developmental process of that culture – to be in its change, rather than seeking to change it.

References

Fanon, F. (1965) *The Wretched of the Earth.* MacGibbon and Kee.

Fanon, F. (1967) *Black Skin, White Masks.* Grove Press.

Foucault, M. (1977) *Discipline and Punish: Birth of the Prison.* Viking.

Goffman, E. (1959) *The Presentation of Self in Everyday Life.* Doubleday.

Guevara, C. (1969) *Guerrilla Warfare.* Pelican.

Illich, I. (1976) *Limits to Medicine: Medical Nemesis: The Expropriation of Health.* Marion Boyars.

Pennant, C. (2008) *Cass.* John Blake.

5

We Don't Need no Education

Calling on some of the areas addressed in previous chapters the following will use personal life history and practice experience to look at and critique the activity of the youth worker in the community. Oft made assumptions about client 'lack of self esteem', 'vulnerability' and 'at risk' status will be questioned before referring to Illich and his ideas about 'de-schooling' as a means of problematising professional incursions (intervention). The potential for the promotion of notions like 'trust' and 'honesty' as part of the professional role will be examined. The efficacy of the youth worker as educator will be broached, leading to an exploration of a perhaps more dynamic attitude to the professional role wherein the youth worker can become a learner, being taught about their practice by those they work with and amongst. Considering Laing, I will the look at the potential to move away from categorisation of clients to a consciousness of the potential individuals and groups have to use situations to develop and educate themselves.

To paraphrase L.P. Hartley, 'the past is a foreign land, they do things differently there'. At one time 'community educators' or youth workers didn't exist. Historians of both these disciplines apparently like to fantasise that other roles in previous centuries can be taken as equivalents. This is crude caricature and crass historical anthropomorphism; just as Noah's Ark was not a cross between a zoo and a cruise liner, a youthful Neanderthal picking up skills to track a wildebeest by hanging round with experienced hunters was not taking part in informal education. A penny farthing was not a form of superbike, no matter how much a cycling historian might want it to be.

In 1967 (the past) youth workers were around, but not where I was. I was actually in a 'foreign land' and they did things differently there, although that time and that place continue to teach me about things happening here and now.

I was 12 years old when Celtic came to Uruguay for the play off to decide whether they or Racing Club Buenos Aires would make the 'Intercontinental Cup', the world cup of club football, their own. While in Montevideo, Celtic stayed at the Victoria Plaza hotel. This was a comparatively chic building and alongside local kids I spent hours outside hoping to catch a glimpse of the players when they first arrived. However, when they did turn up, we got more time to look at them than we expected.

Just a few weeks more than three years later, in London's East End, I would watch the 'Boyos' play against my own team, West Ham United, at the home of the Irons, Upton Park. That was the testimonial evening for the captain of all the Hammers (past and future), patron saint of the claret and blue Docklands, Bobby

Moore. On that November Monday evening in 1970, just as in 1967, I was struck by how big the Scotsmen were and how they looked even more so alongside their own 'Wee Jimmy' Johnstone and West Ham's diminutive Young England international winger (who would score in the 3–3 draw) Johnny Aryis.

The day Celtic arrived in Uruguay the newspapers were preoccupied with the report that the president of the country had challenged his former foreign minister to a duel and taken some holiday to prepare himself for the showdown. Duelling had been against the law in Uruguay from 1909. Legal restraints had been put on another president a few years before, after he and his defence minister had made arrangements to attempt to murder each other.

The Scots got to the hotel to find that their rooms were not available. It seems the Glaswegians were told that an unusual number of prostitutes had been recently seen in the hotel and that there was the potential that the Celtic players would be 'compromised' by the business girls. According to the Scottish Football Association they did not 'put anything past' the Argentine clubs. With the exception of their Manager Jock Stein, the Celtic officials were observant Catholics, so Jock made arrangements to immediately brief his players of the situation.

I had been in Montevideo for nearly six months. I had been due to return to school in September, but that had proved impossible given my father's commitments in Uruguay, but I was, of course, not complaining. Dad had been helping his uncle, Bronco, set up a transport business operating out of the city. Bronco had first come to Uruguay with his father William and, as a boy, had met Isabelino Gradín, a great Argentinean soccer international of the past. This history fascinated me. He would recall Isabelino's black eyes that looked like cool, deep wells and seemed to see right through you. According to Bronco, who as a youth had worn the Celtic colours and later played professional football in Uruguay and Colombia, Gradín seemed to his boyhood mind to know everything about the world within a world that Uruguay was. Bronco, ever the romantic, and a man who fell in love with Uruguay from his earliest years, told me, 'Gradín was part of the living heart of this country. When you knew Gradín, you knew Uruguay.'

Look back on your own childhood and it's likely you'll find someone like Bronco in that place in your personal history, someone who inclined you to think about other people and places, other times and contexts. These are generally not professionals, employed and directed by job descriptions and organisational policy. The people that pass on their insight and wisdom, those who make the fuel for our development of wisdom, tend to be more enduring figures, not bound by the length of a working session or the restrictions of a 'role'. Each of us has at least something of this resource. However, when I listen to youth workers pontificating on how they act as informal and/or community educators, it sometimes seems like they have never really taken the opportunity to know something of the individual and collective wisdom that almost certainly exists in any local social system. It's as though often we enter the places where we work with the assumption that this is a realm of relative ignorance populated almost unquestionably with folk who are 'poorly informed', who require us to educate them. This supposition is clear in the commonly heard aim that we work with people in order that they can make 'informed choices'; how do we know that they are not informed? How do we know that our 'information' is what they need to make their 'choices' or that this 'informing' is any more accurate and meaningful than the information sources already available to them?

As a boy, outside school hours I worked (from the age of six) evenings, weekends and school holidays in my dad's business for pocket money. But also because it was a tradition in my family for children to do what they could to enhance the family income. Everyone always worked at any opportunity. This was expected and insisted upon. No one in the family knew any other family member past or present who had been idle. Even family holidays were spent hop picking, getting up before dawn to work the vines. I was very close to my dad. As a child I spent a great deal of time watching him work deals, but often he would take time in his day to find a quiet street where we'd park the lorry and he'd read me the likes of Dickens, H.G. Wells, Edgar Allen Poe, or Bram Stoker. He was an exciting man. Although he gambled heavily, he had a knack of making money almost from nothing, seemingly able to read minds, picking up on the fear, anxiety or over confidence in other people's faces and actions; to me he was a wizard, cunning but full of humour and able to weave spells from his own aura of silky, dark arrogance. My dad, six foot three, swarthy skinned and black haired, was a devastatingly charming and social person. He was a hugely physically strong man, with bronzed muscles, and seemed to be able to overcome the world, not so much by way of his physical capabilities, more with his mind. He was a swift thinker, with a devastating sense of humour and a massive intellect. I can truly say I've never met a sharper more affable person. I suppose I regarded him as much as my hero friend or big, all protecting brother as a father.

For all this, I guess today I would have been considered to be 'vulnerable'. Indeed the future would confirm any notion (if one had been made) that I was 'at risk'. Dad and I had been through a lot together; his drug addiction, bankruptcy and separation from my mother to mention but a few devastating issues. I suppose he had learnt to depend on me about as much as I did on him. There were grim moments when his mood would become violent and threatening and there was a lot of physical, emotional and psychological trauma for us both in all that. But in all my life I have never stopped loving him and through it all, even in the most awful moments, I knew he loved me. His hurting me hurt him much more. However, we got through it and in that journey I became stronger and discovered my spiritual self. My boyhood life has stood me in good stead when working with others in similarly bleak situations to that which my dad and me inhabited at times. I don't know that any professional could have 'helped' me in those circumstances, or whether an intervening adult would have been 'supportive'. I never felt the need for such a figure. I always thought he and I would get through what we had to. It has to be said, we did. And till the day he passed away I was grateful to have him as my dad.

When I first read *Deschooling Society* by Ivan Illich it reminded me that I had got through my youth without professional incursions, apart from the police of course, but they never hinted they were going to be 'there for me', 'befriend me' or 'educate me'; the cops were always very honest, right down to their big black boots. I've always appreciated police uniforms. When one approaches, you have no doubt about what they want. It's the same with vicars and priests with their dog collars. Both were always very keen to save my soul in one way or another, one by punishment, the other via redemption. However, as a teenager, these amounted to much the same thing, but the old Bill were more interesting and were less inclined to give up than the sky-pilots. Youth workers sort of fell between the two and for the most part were dismissed by both myself and my peers as 'wankers'. A response it has always been useful to remember when, as a youth worker myself, I have started to preach about how much young people were influenced by what we say as professionals. The notion that we should never impose our opinions on or give advice to young people is something of a commandment in youth work (which is odd as it is telling you not to tell people things) but the truth is that most young people are far more likely to do the exact opposite of any instruction I or any other youth worker might inadvertently or purposely give.

It is strange, because not giving advice when someone asks for it is probably more invasive than just answering the best one can. We talk a lot about trust and honesty in our work, but dodging questions about one's opinion or replying to a question with another questions like 'what do you think?' as a constant feels less than honest and is probably unlikely to inspire trust in the questioned questioner. Just imagine that you are waiting for a bus and you ask someone, who you see has a watch, what time it is and they reply 'What time do you think it is?' They then proceed to go through a ritual with you of how you might find out the time for yourself without being dependent on others to tell you the time. I put this scenario to a young woman I was working with and she said 'that bloke with the watch deserves a slap'. I couldn't disagree and of course my boyhood prejudice about youth work practice was at least momentarily confirmed.

Despite this mantra about resisting giving advice and opinion, we seem ready to append labels to people, such as 'at risk', 'vulnerable', assess that they 'lack self esteem' and proceed to treat them in a way that suggests that the labels are in fact truth. Even if we are skilled or qualified enough social psychologists or psychiatrists to make such assessments, we might only see a person in a very limited context, maybe for a couple of hours a week and then usually as part of a bigger group. Few clinical specialists would risk 'treatment' on such a limited experience of another person.

Throughout my youth work career there seems to be at least as much skill in avoiding being invasive in terms of other people's experience as there is in taking opportunities to label someone as 'vulnerable' as a means to make them an object of my 'professional attention', seeing myself as not only a potential but an actual 'helper' or 'supporter'. From my earliest years in the profession I found myself asking how much of this sort of activity in practice creates vulnerability (or conjures it up). After reading another Illich book, *Disabling Professions* it seemed to me that my questioning was vindicated

Before going to Uruguay my father had never been abroad, but I had been to America with an uncle a few years previously and I think this was something of a psychological support for the old man and maybe part of the reason (perhaps unconscious) why he thought he would take me to what was such a strange land at that time.

Montevideo was a fascinating place for me. I grew to love the Biblioteca Nacional del Uruguay, in Casilla de Correo and it was there, via a friendly English speaking librarian that I found out the city's full original name was 'San Felipe y Santiago de Montevideo' and there are a few ideas of what *Montevideo* means. One of the most common interpretations is that it comes from the Portuguese 'Monte vide eu' meaning 'I see a mountain'. Another argument goes that the Spaniards recorded the location of a mountain on a map as 'Monte VI De Este a Oeste' which translates as, 'The sixth mountain from east to west'. But both these explanations give you some idea about the area in which Montevideo is situated.

Montevideo had an underlying complexity and I revelled in the fading but fabulous ethos of the Old Town (Ciudad Vieja) with its quaint combination of colonial Spanish, Italian and Art Deco styles. With buildings going back to the 18th century, it was contrasted by the vibrant Mercado del Puerto, which fascinated me with its odd amalgamation of busyness set in a relaxed atmosphere. Montevideo is not by any means a beautiful city architecturally, although I didn't know that then. This was before I'd seen Venice or Rome, Quebec or Hong Kong. My 'natural habitat' was post-war, inner-cityscape. I grew up playing on bomb sites and with the enchantment of places where industrial landscapes coalesced with the rough borders between urban and rural. A river which had been denuded of the industry that adorned my environment like a living crown lured me to its banks and inlets; my boyhood was spent exploring great swathes of no-mans-land and these places are still where my dreams take place. As such, Montevideo was a new poetry for me, but probably its intriguing stanzas were the magic of its people.

My relationship with cities has always symbolised what I have grown to see as my personal freedom. Yes, my amblings though these places were probably risky and even dangerous expeditions, often trotting and jumping though tumble down buildings and disused docks. But I didn't want a 'safe environment' of the type I so often hear that professionals have 'built' for their 'clients' where they can 'just be themselves'. Can anyone 'be themselves' in such situations? I was lucky enough to spend some time with R.D. Laing when I first became interested in working with people when he was operating in Aldgate, East London. His ideas and writing have constantly informed and reminded me about the experience of professional incursions and labelling; how we tend to manufacture 'symptoms' out of defining behaviour in 'artificial' contexts. Laing's work in East London was an effort to remove himself and those he worked with from the professional presence and the 'clinical environment' wherein, to unfairly sum up a number of his books, no one can 'be themselves' as they, quite understandably and naturally, are preoccupied with defending themselves from the often unknown (to them) agenda of professional assaults.

But although Montevideo was a great friend to me, I was nevertheless sometimes a little lonely when my father had to go out of the city on business, when transport or circumstance did not allow me to accompany him to meet Bronco far along the arteries that spread out from the city.

Although most Montivideans had European ancestry, their forbears coming from Italy and Spain, and like the area where I came from there was also significant Jewish and African communities (the latter has grown in recent years), it had unexpected cultural diversity for such a small population, and a character far removed from anything I had experienced. For all this, I loved the freedom I had in what was a very 'child friendly' and relatively safe, strangely handsome city. Even today one can walk around anywhere without much danger, even some of the most run down areas are not bad neighbourhoods. But what is a 'bad neighbour-hood? I've lived in some so called 'bad places' and had a great time.

Likewise I have had recourse to make my home in what is considered to be 'good areas' and have found them almost as deadly boring as the 'safe environments' I have witnessed youth workers providing. I've come to the conclusion that I like what is called 'bad' because things happen in such places – so 'bad' is 'good'? I don't know if I always want to live in 'Murder Zone No.1 East London' but at the same time I don't want to ever live in *Sea Haven* (see http://www.ruinedendings.com/film1331plot).

Uruguay traditionally (arising out of economic necessity) uses buildings for many more years than might be the case in most of Western Europe. I found this habit comforting; it was as if nothing really died in the place; people breathed life into things and places and by an act of collective will the streets and alleyways held the energy of renewal and that latent power found in the sacred potential of resurrection. To that extent Montevideo, for me, had a secular holiness, the ether was laced by care.

Left to my own devices, with the city's attractions open year-round (the climate remains temperate and mild, even in winter) I would roam unfettered. One of my favourite places was the La Feria Tristán Narvaja, a Sunday morning Flea Market on the Tristán Narvaja Street. At the entrance people would sell puppies and I still wonder what happened to the ones that didn't get sold.

I would wander round the city's many parks (some people call Montevideo the 'City of Parks') and along its beaches, like Pocitos, Buceo, Malvin, Playa de los Ingleses, Playa Verde, Punta Gorda and Carrasco, which made it feel like you had a seaside resort on your doorstep, although these shores had little in common with the likes of Southend or any British coastal resort, with Argentines and Brazilians visiting in the summer (December to February) to bask on the white sands that are linked by the Rambla waterside roadway. Along this 13.6 mile (22 kilometre) ribbon of life cyclists, drinkers and fishermen made entertaining theatre for the inveterate people watcher I was (a habit I've not given up) and the views out to sea, particularly at sunset, are magical.

It sometimes makes me sad that many – perhaps most – children in the west might miss out on this kind of playground for the mind. 'Positive activities' and 'programmes for betterment' seem anaemic in comparison. Professional intervention sometimes feels like a sharp, cold tool so much so that it suggests there must be an alternative.

In these places I sometimes found football games that I could be part of, and there seemed to be little discrimination as to who might take part. I recall playing with fully grown men, boys older and younger than myself as well as making up the numbers for a girls side. I played a part in quite few matches between two sides made up of very old blokes (more or less the same personnel for every game, they all looked about 100 to me at the time, but I guess most were over 60). They insisted that I changed sides every ten minutes to make it fair; 'Hey Lennox!' they shouted when they wanted the ball or passed it to me, making me proud that they were likening me (with my dark hair and pale skin) to Bobby Lennox, (whose role in winning the European Cup with Celtic had made a mark in Uruguay).

Football in Uruguay is like a form of worship, the sacrament of playing seems available to all who want in; I was altar boy, priest and congregation. The name the old boys gave me stuck and I achieved a modicum of fame as 'pequeño Británico', or 'parvulo Lennox' on the beaches of Uruguayan capital.

It was the old men who first introduced me to Tommy McInally, a former Celtic player whose memory amazingly endured in Montevideo more than forty years after his tour of Argentina and Uruguay with Third Lanark. They taught me this song (sung to the tune of 'Roaming in the Gloamin') even though few had much more English than it took to sing the song:

Tommy McInally,
He's the toast of ground and stand,
Tommy McInally,
He's the greatest in the land,
Even though I get the sack,
How I love my Tommy Mac,
Oh, I love my Tommy McInally!
What a player! What a man!

It is remarkable how we can adapt to our environments even at as younger teenagers, or perhaps particularly at that time of life. There is a time when we seem to be ready or even need to find out more about the world we live in. A lot has been written about the 'stages' of human development, much of it based on western presumptions and contexts, but there is something about humans that they often grow when they need to; finding ourselves in particular circumstances at opportune times, we do have the capacity to respond more or less appropriately and find a way. Watching and accompanying young people with regard and I hope the generosity of consideration I believe they will usually fill the space available to them to grow and often defy the limits of the 'stages' set for them. In one agency I worked with a young man who everyone knew as 'Milky'. He was about four feet tall, tubby with very light skin and white hair. I guess he was somewhere between 10 and 13 years old, but I never met his parents and in the 30 months I was with the project no one mentioned his age although it was probably recorded somewhere.

From the time I started working at the project I got the impression that the other young people had practically adopted Milky. They greeted him 'Alwite Milk!' and generally looked after him. I began to understand from what others told me and his general behaviour that he might be what is called autistic. I had worked with very young children who were given this label years earlier, but my time with Ronnie Laing had caused me to question such categories and I never made any effort to name Milky as anything other than what he said he was, although he actually said very little. Sometimes Milky would rock-up to my office before the club opened, around 4.30 p.m. He would get himself a drink, come into my office and usually sit on the safe where he had a good view of what I was doing. He'd stay there, sometimes ask what I was doing, until others turned up, then he'd just sort of roll around with them, perhaps getting involved in a game of table tennis or football, or just watch the telly eating Rolos or Mars Bars. At the end of the evening there were always two or three older people who would walk him home. If we organised a trip or if we were involved in a sporting fixture that required travelling to another venue, Milky would always be there, mostly unannounced. At times I'd open the van, go into the club to get the football or netball team and I'd get back to find Milky sitting in his usual seat, as if appearing from nowhere. No one found this unusual. The others would climb in the van . . . 'Alwite Milk!' He just found us and we found him and the 'usness' grew. It was all very natural; Milky was organic.

Montevideo is one of the most important ports in South America and when I was a kid about a third of Uruguay's population lived in the city. About ten per cent lived in the province of Canelones, which might be understood as the outlying neighbourhoods of the city that merge into rural suburbs. Now Montevideo is the only city in Uruguay to have a population over a million, but while I was there it seemed to be much less crowded than the cityscapes I was familiar with.

One thing that connected me with something I knew was the national love of football and Nacional, arguably the best club in the country at the time (Peñarol fans will be the most quarrelsome on this point) became something of a means for me to acclimatise to the place. This allegiance was fired by my meeting with José Pedro Cea. When I met José he was approaching his 68th year. My great uncle had introduced him to my dad and me. He was a former Nacional player and Uruguay's leading goalscorer in the 1930 FIFA World Cup. He scored the crucial equalising goal in the World Cup final against Argentina, levelling the score to 2–2 in the 57th minute. He looked a proud and dignified man and it seemed that everyone had a story about Cea, either connected with matches he played for Nacional or his games in a Uruguayan shirt. He was not a legend like his Nacional colleague Hector Scarone, but he was certainly a local hero and a man held in the highest esteem for both his football and the way he led his life. After meeting him Nacional would always be my team in South America.

People make places, places make people. We tend to reflect on who we are through the people we've known, the places we've been. We become who we are through interactions with others in particular contexts, and generally speaking, the wider the context the more we become whatever it is that makes us. We can't know everybody but we can look to know everyone we meet to some extent. Youth workers can't change the world but the world does change youth workers, their practice and the way they see things and this causes changes in the world. So if you feel your practice hardly changes there is a message to be read in this. If you read this book and insist on not reconsidering your practice you might as well never have read this book, but if you don't reconsider your practice it is likely that you haven't really read this book.

The project where I worked with Milky (or where he worked with me) was a borderland of football support. The area met in a sort of apex of territory between West Ham United, Tottenham Hotspurs and Arsenal (these were the days when people still supported the team in their area – there were really no 'Cockney Reds' to speak of, and few Chelsea fans did not have some definite connection with SW6). The agency I worked for was based right on Virginia Circus in Bethnal Green, a stones throw from Petticoat Lane market. Most of the young people lived on the old London County Council estate that made up that particular part of the world. These were sturdily built brown tenements, each block stood alongside others forming tight circles around a series of courtyards. The area was once known as the 'Nickel' and was at the centre of the district named locally as the 'Jago', at one time it was a 'no-go' area for the police and more or less self-ruled. It was probably the toughest part of tough East London at that point. A few minutes walk away was Valance Road, home of the Kray Twins.

The day after I left the project I was taken out by some of the older members and staff to several of the local pubs. It was early morning before we got back to the main part of the estate where most of the people I worked with lived. I admit I was quite drunk. We stood in the middle of the courtyard saying our goodbyes and suddenly all the lights in the kitchens and doorways of the surrounding blocks were turned on. Suddenly we were standing in the middle of a huge, brightly lit amphitheatre. People were out on the walkways at every level; whole families, clapping and chanting my name to a popular football support rhythm . . . clap, clap . . . clap, clap, clap . . . clap, clap, clap, CLAP . . . Belton! Right at the top of the flats, sitting with his feet daggling out of a rooftop window was Milky . . . just being Milky . . . how he had always been all the time I had been with the project. We often talk about what we put into our jobs, but my guess is that we get much more out than we put in if we just 'go with' people. Milky had in him all he needed to become all he could be and what he was, was much, much more than good enough. He was beautiful and I could not, with any effort of mine, 'educate' him or make him 'better'. In fact Milky educated me.

During my time in Montevideo I had not had any chance to attend a top football match and had only seen the great and historic El Centenario stadium from the outside. You might be able to imagine my reaction to my father telling me Pedro Cea had got him tickets to see Celtic play Racing Club in the playoff for the Intercontinental Cup at that wondrous venue the day before what for us was Guy Fawkes Day, just a week prior to the date we were due to make our way back to Britain. I couldn't believe it. I stared at the tickets on the table in the room we had close to Plaza Matriz. They looked insubstantial relative to the promises they carried. Looking back now, over 40 years on, it still seems impossible. A star, a goal scorer, in the winning side of the first World Cup had got us tickets to see Celtic play Racing Club in another world championship, the first ever contested by a British side. I felt I had been blessed by an angel of football; my dreams in the nights before the game were full of irretrievable but remarkable conversations with Isabelino Gradín (once in the form of a Geoffrey's Cat!) and incarnations of incorporeal consciousness of Uruguay.

Getting into the stadium was hard work. Police searched every spectator for knives and other weapons at the turnstiles and while my dad and I were waiting we saw about a dozen people refused entry. We were high up in the Amsterdam stand and it took my dad and I ages to scale the stairs in the vast crowd. We then had to find our seats, which was another task, as many of the rows weren't marked. It was just a case of finding a place where you didn't get jostled into a less favourable position in terms of view of the pitch, although looking back the sight lines of the stadium were unfaultable.

The authorities in Uruguay had tried to make the venue as neutral as possible but as we looked out over the vast crowd it was easy to see that the majority were Racing supporters. However, as I watched in awe, I estimated that although not all were Glaswegian Celtic fans, about half of the 75,000 present were throwing their support behind the European champions in preference to the despised traditional foe. Racing had beaten Nacional in the final of the *Copa Libertadores* earlier in the year and this denied the people of Montevideo the chance of a crack at becoming known as the home of the world's best football team. The two matches of that final had epitomised the worst type of sporting attrition and Racing's victory in the eventual playoff in Santiago, Chile had left a bitter taste in the mouth of most Uruguayans. So much so one of the biggest groups in the stadium were the police. The authorities had been so worried about possible violence that an armed policeman was in every tenth seat. I later heard that around two thousand riot police were deployed in and around the stadium.

Of course the match programme was written in Spanish, but I saw that the referee was Dr Rodolfo Osorio. Celtic would not have been unhappy to have the same Uruguayan officials that 'controlled' the second leg game in Buenos Aires, both the players and the manager thought that Esteban Marino and his linesmen (sounds like a Latino Punk band) had done what they could to manage that game in an even handed way in what had been a particularly intimidating atmosphere, but the regulations of the competition prevented the use of the same group of officials; referees and linesmen from the host country were disallowed. So the playoff was managed by a tubby 29 year old geezer from Paraguay.

A few years ago I was in hospital recovering from a life threatening illness and received a telephone call. It was from Steven Smith, like myself a West Ham supporter. He was one of the people I had worked with at the project in Bethnal Green some 25 years earlier. He had got my number from West Ham (I had done a lot of work with West Ham in the Community over the previous few years). Steve hadn't known I was ill and had just phoned to find out if I was 'Alwite'.

But this was not really about Steve and me, or me and that project. It says something of how we can build networks of enduring care, not by efforts to make people 'better' or to 'educate' them but by knowing and understanding that they already have what they need to be whole. Our honour as workers is that we might have the time and hopefully the ability to be with people as they become what they need and want to be; to stand with them and by them and have them stand by us. Youth work is a 'growth' industry but growth is as dependent on 'not doing' when appropriate at least as much as 'doing' when required.

However, if people are to grow around us we need to be ready to grow with them; development is necessarily about give and take. Taking is as important as giving because taking allows others to give; giving and having what you give accepted is a concrete acknowledgement that one is regarded as a human being. Giving is at least as rewarding as taking. Effective youth workers know how to give and take and when to give and when to take what is given with grace and appreciation. That is a noble and honourable model of being.

I often smile inwardly when someone tells me they learn best from experience. I have yet to find out how anything can be learnt or lived outside experience. I took much from my experience of Montevideo and I brought this back in Bethnal Green, but at the same time I added my experience of Uruguay to my experience of the people at the heart of that old LCC estate. None of this was very 'safe'. A narrow escape from death brought Bethnal Green back to me and much of the reason for what has been my life. Our lives are worthy to be looked back on for in them is all we know and all we are – how can we know others unless we are prepared to get to know ourselves better? Our experiences are our bridges to the future. As such every experience we have with young people is potentially a precious moment for them as these experiences link who they are with the people they might become. But they are also our experiences and they connect us with them so much so that phone calls come from decades ago into the now. We define, we make each other. I seek the advice of those I work with to do what I can do as well as I can. I value and want their opinions. But why would they give me advice unless I am prepared to take that chance and offer the same to them? Why give your opinion to someone not prepared to give you their own in return – 'give' being the operative word.

Professionals ask young people to give information about their sex life, family situation, friends, their telephone number, age, home address, ethnicity, but it is rare that this will be more than a one-way requirement – this sort of data is not gained as part of an information exchange. They do not have, and so cannot share, records of all the professionals they come into contact with. No one in Montevideo interrogated me in the way I see professions routinely questioning young people in the UK, but I was openly interrogated by the people I worked with in Bethnal Green, and probably quite rightly. After all, as they often reminded me, I was the one getting paid and the one getting their time, commitment and trust. But that trio of honours were given because I gave to them, part of this giving was the information about myself. People who require trust from others can keep few secrets from those same people – else what would their trust be based on? But that is all far from 'safe'. In fact, like all things in life worth having, it is shot-through with 'risk'. Most people do not fall into the category of being 'vulnerable' and if one does see everyone as relatively vulnerable, not only is that vaguely patronising, it is very much seeing the cup as 'half-empty'. Unless our lives have been a series of terrifying experiences we will not look back on the 'safe times' as the great times. The most fabulous and self-actualising moments will be those that were 'unsafe' and 'risky'. Like being in Montevideo on my own when I was 12, like being with my dad, like being drunk in the Jago, like Milky on the rooftops, a place where he could see everything, shining white like one of the stars in the dark, dark blue skies over East London.

References

Belton, B. (2008) *The Battle of Montevideo.* History Press.

Guevara, C. (1961) *Guerrilla Warfare.* M R Press.

Hartley, L.P. (1953) *The Go-Between.* Hamish Hamilton.

http://wwwruinedendings.com/film1331plot

Laing, R.D. (1970) *Sanity, Madness and the Family.* Pelican.

Laing, R.D. (1970) *The Divided Self.* Pelican.

Laing, R.D. (1971) *Self and Others.* Pelican.

Illich, I. (1971) *Deschooling Society.* Harper and Row.

Illich, I. (1977) *Disabling Professions.* M Boyars.

6

From the Matrix to Conviviality and Eutrapelia

The ideas developed in this chapter were inspired by *Tools for Conviviality* by Ivan Illich, and the work of Noam Chomsky, some of whose ideas have been called on directly to provoke consideration of how international politics and economics impact on and question localised youth work practice.

I will look at the future potential for dialectical relations and continue questioning of previous chapters about the practice of informal education and its appropriateness as a youth work tool. In the light of this I will formulate different tactics of association, calling on Illich's *Disabling Professions* I will go on to critique 'compassion' as a basis of practice and examine the 'splintering specialisation' experienced in youth work.

The chapter will then turn more directly to Chomsky and his critique of modern state and foreign policy. This will cause an examination of how global conditions have brought many of what have been understood as basic tasks of youth work – 'community action', 'empowerment' and 'informal education' and, in particular, ambitions around youth worker promotion and implementation of democratic attitudes and structures, into question.

In exploring parallels between Andy and Larry Wachowski's *The Matrix* and the contemporary situation and the role of the media, I will consider informal education and covert indoctrination and what is called 'protection' as a means of surveillance.

Developing Illich's notion of 'graceful playfulness' and Guevara's theory of guerrilla warfare the chapter will conclude with some ideas about developing the direction of practice given the previous analysis.

Ivan Illich was a pastor in South America and it was from this setting that he framed his thinking around alternative technologies. He was one of the first prolific writers in the post-war period to believe that the world could not sustain modern industrial growth, or more particularly, the relations that this growth engenders. His ideas are pertinent to youth workers thinking about themselves as professionals working in the community as he insists that healthy, nourishing, interpersonal and communal relationships are not possible given the nature of our society, it being based on growth and the continued generation of material wealth and consumerism. Chomsky is an important linguist and critic of US foreign policy. Born two years after Illich (in 1928) he is Professor of Linguistics at the Massachusetts Institute of Technology, in Cambridge Massachusetts. The importance of Chomsky in the field of linguistics is summed up by the much repeated contention that there have only been two stages in the development of theoretical linguistics – BC and AD, Before Chomsky and After his Discoveries. His approach to US foreign policy in the post Second World War period has been a constant thorn in the side of successive American administrations with regard to their international dealings. He has written a plethora of books on this subject.

Illich, the professions and industrialisation

For Illich the professions, which have had a major role in supporting industrialisation and the technological society, are no longer able to cope with the strains placed upon them. Hence, social workers, nurses, doctors, police and youth workers are, as individuals, and collectively as professions, buckling under the strain of the demands put upon them by inequality and the increasingly impervious division between those in poverty and the rest of society. This will ring very true for many professionals struggling to make a difference in the context of the community.

Illich believes that in time the professions will vanish. For instance, for him universal education through compulsory schooling is not possible on a global basis. Although it would be impossible for any government to admit as much, it has long been unrealistic in the British context, for example, to expect every child to be given like access to educational resources. As this becomes more and more obvious, it is also increasingly plain (even though the state continues to raise the school leaving age) that the idea of long years of education are not what everybody wants or needs; notions like 'life long learning', 'community education' and 'informal education' have no real applicability or demand outside of state ambitions to produce a relatively cheap, relatively flexible workforce in the face of competition from emerging economies for capitalist investment.

Electronic media has been put forward as the alternative or companion to schooling that will make the classroom and the school more malleable resources, perhaps eventually having the muscle to do away with the concrete institutional structure altogether. 'Virtual' universities already exist, but even in the infancy of such innovation it is proving to be destructive of fundamental values of interaction and collaborative communal life, isolating individuals who, bathed in the stark light of a computer screen, find the notion of cooperation a remote and even alien concept that many experience difficulty in relating to having been weaned on the essentialist consumerism premised on lonely individualism. Indeed, the internet is much more a facility for the use of global capitalism and militarism than a replacement for educational institutions; by far the biggest hit numbers coagulate around the tumultuous helpings of cyber pornography that grow by the commercialised minute. Some have even argued that without the money generated by pornography, we would have no internet. As such, it is clear that electronic media (including mobile telephone technology) are limited to providing 'information' and a platform for 'dialoguing' at best. They restrict related interaction to the level of the message, and do not create an environment for shared human consideration, association or regard in any appreciable measure beyond sectional and cult interests. This is most certainly confirmed after consideration of the relations they undermine. They probably also erode the potential to achieve meaningful dialectical relationships as the nature of the media means that thoughts are more swapped than shared. In the 'twitism' context this is confirmed by the limit on the length of 'tweets' – communication and expression might be extended laterally but it is curtailed in terms of depth and meaning.

Like education, it has also become obvious that a full range of medical commodities cannot be made available generally. Divisions in health and health care are evident even within the states of the West (Britain and the US, for example).

So we, as professionals in the community, cannot rely on what have become to be understood as the means of supplying of informal education. Local authorities and government simply do not have the resources to meet the need; it is impossible for inner London boroughs, for example, with youth populations of tens of thousands to 'meet the needs of young people' in their district, maybe deploying a score or two full-time workers (at most) and several dozen part-time staff. Even bolstered by a few hundred volunteers, the lack of facilities show the enterprise to be massively under-resourced. We also are unable to look to technology to help us out. If Illich is right, the club, the project, the youth agency, the mini-bus and the general outlook of youth workers, as we know them, are no longer appropriate in their present social form. The current children and young people strategy, that in essence has the ambition to produce a minimally skilled, more numerous (and so comparatively cheap) work force, looks hopelessly inadequate.

The central problem with current intentions and general tactics is that they are deeply flawed, being connected to commodity based social enterprise. The growing popularity of the term 'social capital' reflects this, albeit unconsciously perhaps. All the ideology and dogma of 'social' or 'community action', 'democracy', 'informal education' and 'empowerment' has been proved false as it is obvious to even the cursory observer that the effects of the same are minimal, being applied to a minority of the youth population. This being the case, there is a need to formulate different tactics of association and action.

Illich observed that the professions that grew out of industrial society shared a common trait with other mega-enterprises. Growth, beyond a certain point, frustrates the end which was originally intended. At this moment the entity then becomes a threat to society. In books like *Disabling Professions* Illich has claimed that modern medicine, for example, has done more to make people ill than provide widespread forms of health, in that it requires a vast industrial and commercial structure to allow it to operate. The Union Carbide tragedy in Bhopal, India in 1982 was an example of the harm that is part and parcel of the chemical industry. The exploitation that was exposed underpins medical enterprise. Still, vaccines are sent to non-industrial countries, by way of aid or purchase agreements with industrialised states, which have no chance of use given that (for example) appropriate refrigeration is not available. On a global scale, human immunity to disease has been eroded by the wide and indiscriminate use of antibiotics. These are just a couple of examples of how the growth of the medical industry has had detrimental effects for huge numbers of people.

In the same way, mass social work has cut people off from supportive relations motivated by love, respect and regard, the notion of welfare rights have replaced familial or community ideas of duty. Human rights have become no more than a form of at best placebo used to quell discontent and at worst a means of promoting commercial interests. Paying tax or insurance to pay for social humanitarian services effectively alienates the cared for from the carer and replaces this with forms of contract and 'right'. Those in need of care are increasingly 'the other'. And as the social resources, that once kept the abstracted forms of care going, dwindle it seems that we, as a society may have forgotten or lost the skills and attitudes of a more personal means of care. Once the vast mass of people cared for (laid out and buried) their own dead. Now the very idea of coping with the disposal of our loved ones without the aid of the undertaking industry would be an anathema. Our old are placed in inadequate facilities that are closer to forms of punishment than care, which disturbingly fits in with the 'botoxification' of our external selves; poison injected in the face to ward off the perceived sin of age.

Even if it were possible for professional forms of care to be extended to all, it could not replace familial or more 'organic' relations where compassion is the driving force.

Compassion

For all this, writers and practitioners in a number of ways have claimed that compassion is the 'kernel' of professional practice. Despite our obvious connection with control agenda we continue to insist the basis of what we do is founded on 'support' and 'helping'. We may help people in our work and have compassion for some of those we come into contact with, but is that central to our job? Is it generally included in job descriptions for instance? Even if it is, how would we make sure that we recruit the most compassionate people? How might we make a fair and accurate judgment about people's comparative capacity for compassion? Is compassion a 'one way thing'? Some might feel that to share in someone's suffering (this is what 'compassion' means) that the person on the 'sharp end' (receiving compassion) needs to allow this to happen; do the people we work with and for want this? Have they requested this?

Can we provide compassion to all those we come across in our work every day of our working lives? Is compassion quantifiable? What resources would be necessary? Do we have the spiritual and emotional energy for such a massive task? What about empathy? Do we, can we and should we give both empathy and compassion? How about sympathy? How much compassion, empathy and sympathy do we have or give? Do we take the homeless (all of them) home if we can't find them a roof over their head one evening? That might be understood as 'sharing suffering'. How would an employer, funder or inspector make sure that those they employ, fund or inspect are 'giving out' sufficient and apposite compassion?

At what stage does compassion become unsuitable? One might have compassion for someone who is brutally attacked, but can one have compassion for the assailant at the same time? If we can this does not mean that everyone working in the field can (or should). Are we better or worse at our jobs according to where we are on some indistinct scale of 'compassion distribution'? One person's compassion can be another's inhumanity or patronisation – some feel it is compassionate to help the terminally ill to die, others believe that this is no better than cold blooded murder – who will decide, in terms of practice standards, what is and what isn't compassionate?

If we make the 'sharing of suffering' a priority of our practice, those subscribing to the ideas and theories of psychoanalysis might see us as being at risk of 'transference' (out of control compassion?). This begs the question, can we 'over-identify' with those we work with, to the extent that we are seeing our unique and personal experience being the same as their exceptional circumstances (and vice versa)? This could be thought of as the colonialisation of another's feelings.

The same order of questioning arises when we look at the consequences of making helping 'central' to our role. How much 'help' should a professional give? How do we know if we have given enough help? How do we decide to distribute this help and who to? Can we help everyone or even everyone with the same problems? Seeing someone as in need of help is to see them as being more or less helpless (evoking pity; they are seen as pitiful). Is this not something of the same sort of deficit model applied in colonial situations that were/are often more about control than help?

The proposal that professionals make compassion central is similar to that of the informal educator – a clear practice agenda that prescribes what it is we should and should not do, calling more on opinion than any hard evidence. While laying out instructions for us (and the world) there is an insistence that we should not have agenda for others. Might the less charitable reader understand this position as at least confused and contradictory or at worse hypocritical and manipulative? Is it fostering anything more than an elaborate deficit model that sees professionals as potentially being great fonts of compassion and education and others ('clients') as pitiful and ignorant and constant recipients of our ubiquitous 'love' and 'compassion' that knows no bounds? Does this risk making us something like the missionaries of colonial times, voyaging to far away places to bring our 'gifts' to those who do not know the rewards of our sacrifice? Who does this give power to?

In the last analysis is it not the case that our role has an inherent expectation that we logically, rationally and cost effectively, manage and deliver, first and foremost, welfare and care resources and services, while promoting governmental interpretations of education (best practice)? Is not our work primarily concerned with efforts to extend, as best we can, fairness and justice, rather than importing indeterminist sentiment that does little more than confuse issues and roles, while serving to cloud coordinated judgement?

Harsh critics may accuse those who portray themselves as bottomless wells of compassion or 'suppliers of an endless diet of help' or 'education' as being not professionally coherent, but rather suffering from an overblown professional ego involving a desire to be understood as a sort of streetwise saint, a 'saviour' of those we work with. Would we be better understanding the 'kernel' of our work being humane diligence and attentive focus?

But for all the alleged 'professional compassion' never, in any society, have there been so many lonely people, often festering in poverty, sickness or disability. In Illich's words, people have been locked into 'a man-made shell'.

Splintering specialisation

At the same time, the very texture of the local social networks that we call community has been undermined by the promotion of social polarisation and splintering specialisation. That is, groups have been separated into gender, cultural, ethnic, sexuality, intellectual, age or class types or categories and this is secured by specialists (education/welfare professionals) making one or a selection of these categories their 'specialist'. This specialisation functions together with the institutionalisation of values ('schools should teach the difference between right and wrong'), gives rise to the centralisation of power/authority (people are split into competing factions for social resources rather than amalgamated as individuals and groups able to take authority over their lives). At this point, for Illich, people become 'accessories of bureaucracies or machines'. They are made objects or things to be treated according to prescribed rules. Needs are homogenised and uniqueness undermined in the treatment. The bureaucratic process of 'equal opportunities' is an example of this practice; our morality is checked out according to prescribed criteria and we 'pass or fail' the test of policy and legislation rather than be trusted to our own and the collective moral compass to achieve the more pertinent equality of outcome.

Chomsky, the role of the media and the use of language in shaping the perceptions of foreign policy

This situation is elaborated by Chomsky. He argues that the media and the intellectual community shape terminology to the interests of power. Any word used in political discourse has at least two meanings, a dictionary meaning and a meaning used for ideological warfare. Democracy, a system or an idea that youth work places central to its cause, has a dictionary meaning, which will refer to a population taking part in the rule of a state in some meaningful way. The democratic state, as understood by the ideological elite, is a state that is dominated by the business class. The general public in such a state are merely 'spectators' – they are not participants. Their activity in terms of political power is restricted to being occasionally allowed to pull a lever or make a mark on a ballot paper. After this they go back to their spectator role. If the public do enter into the political system, then there is, what the political elites call, 'a crisis of democracy', presenting a predicament that must be overcome and the population returned to their apathy and obedience. This complies with a well reasoned theory that is articulated at great length in the academic literature that is, as Harold Laswell (1905) put it:

> *People are not the best judges of their own interest . . . that is the democratic dogmatism . . . 'We' are the best judges of their interests. So for their benefit we have to protect society from 'the ignorant and meddlesome outsiders', or else there will be trouble . . .*

That's democracy. As you may be able to see, international relations, although seemingly remote from the day-to-day activity of professional practice and the lives of those we work with and among, have a crucial impact on the nature of youth work as so many of its fundamental precepts are caught up in the effects of macro-political circumstances. National and international policy, legislation and economics affect funding and organisational aims and, as such, to purposely ignore – or fail to attempt – an understanding of the events and situations that create our practice environment, is actually indulging in resolute ignorance. That said, political studies play a relatively small part in youth work training. I recently accompanied a group of undergraduate students on a field trip to the Houses of Parliament, a significant number of them had very little idea of the function, structure or workings of government. A subsequent visit by a final year group revealed an even more noticeable level of naivety as well as appreciable apathy.

A traditional backdrop to so called 'democratic' societies has been free markets. Britain is one of the 'market democracies', an essential aspect of capitalism that are generally taken to be models of the ideal state in capitalist economic thinking. The first lesson that is taught in economics is that free trade maximises the efficient use of resources and few in government would oppose that. Yet in the real world, no wealthy society ever subjects itself to market discipline, unless there is some accidental or conditional advantage to it. Any regulation that exists is put in place to maximise profit – tax rates deal with any potential or actual loss. If you didn't see or believe this before the credit crunch perhaps you will now. But the history of Britain or the US or any other industrialised society demonstrates that they develop by essentially defying the precepts of the free market economics.

Had America during the 1820s stuck to the notion of efficient use of resources, it would still be exporting fur. But the USA created high tariff areas to stop cheap British exports to generate its own textile industry. The steel industry in America was created by a similar strategy. This process has continued for almost 200 years and continues today. In the late 1990s computers and semi-conductors were the focus.

Historically, Britain, deploying the same tactics, destroyed Indian industry, which was approximately analogous to its own. At the height of the British Empire the development of Egyptian industry was blocked by both economic and colonial force. As soon as Britain knew that it had achieved a position where practically no competition was left, it favoured free markets, but only up to the point when the competition started to recover, at which point the Empire was closed off in terms of free trade. At present France (overtly) and the USA (by stealth) are shutting the doors of free markets. Between championing 'British jobs for British workers' Britain continues to extol free markets, probably because there are no actual 'British jobs' as much of what industry there is in Britain is foreign owned – so the real cry should be 'Chinese jobs for British workers'.

Markets are not for the major industrial powers, they're for other people; market conditions are imposed on the poor. Hence you and I over the next two decades or so will underwrite state gambling debts. The non-industrialised world is obliged, or if necessary compelled, to meet extreme market conditions. This is how language is used. The word 'market' is used to say one thing but it also has an ideological meaning that you have to literally uncover.

Youth work is not immune from this practice. We say we are involved in educating young people, but they rarely know that this is part of our agenda (we use the camouflage of 'fun' etc.). How can someone be educated if they don't know they are being educated? That is a form of indoctrination. The informal predicate confirms this as it usually means 'covert' – the education is not overtly carried out – isn't that propaganda? The label 'informal education' thus analysed equates to a means of covert indoctrination using subtle forms of propaganda. Likewise 'welfare' is control and 'protection' is surveillance and so on.

Our society as such creates understandings that contradict the character of reality. This makes the individual in society psychically disorientated. We instinctively know we really do not know what is happening, but we can only understand what is happening through the explanations we are offered. Particularly in the young, as they discover this, this obliges a retreat to apathy and ultimately irrationality. Morpheus, in Andy and Larry Wachowski's (1999) *The Matrix* offers an insight into this situation:

> *Let me tell you why you're here. You're here because you know something. What you know you can't explain, but you feel it. You've felt it your entire life, that there's something wrong with the world. You don't know what it is, but it's there, like a splinter in your mind, driving you mad. It is this feeling that has brought you to me. Do you know what I'm talking about?*

The Matrix was released in March, 1999 and following its success, two sequels, *The Matrix Reloaded* (May 2003) and *The Matrix Revolutions* (November 2003) made up the series. The settings and characters of the fictional Matrix universe were further elaborated in other media, including comics, animation and video games. The series incorporates a range of philosophical elements, including influences of anime, cyberpunk, mythology, Hong Kong action films (principally 'heroic bloodshed' and martial arts films) philosophy of mind and simulated reality. Several belief systems are touched upon, Hinduism, Buddhism, Jainism, Christianity and Sufism. The film and the world it elaborates provide something of a heuristic device to illustrate the incursions of the state into the everyday life of the individual.

This is the atmosphere within which, we as youth workers, to all intents and purposes, are agents of the same state that contorts language and so truth. We ask young people (as they are discovering this state of affairs) to 'trust' us, in order that we can 'build relationships', not because we want young people as our personal friends or companions but, in the last analysis, in order that we might use these 'relationships' to achieve organisational ends or align our work with state policy and legislation.

Other words with other meanings, even perhaps meanings that are the direct opposite to their meanings as commonly understood are 'democracy', 'freedom' and 'choice'. You can choose what school your children goes to for instance; but this often means that you choose between one failing school and another. We also use words that we have little idea about what they actually mean. 'Community' is one, 'power' is another. Youth and community work has a history of claims of 'empowerment' (giving power) but this of course is a contradiction in terms. If one needs to be given power one has been seen as being powerless – one is understood as not being able to gain power for oneself. At the same time the 'empowerer' logically sees themselves as the holder of power, since how else could they give power?

Most of us are born with the potential to influence our environment to some extent. The extent that we can use this influence to gain authority is the extent to which we have 'social control' over our environment. So power can be taken as the use of influence to gain authority to take control (to some extent) of our lives and contexts. But 'power' is hardly ever explained in these terms. For most of us power is taken to be amorphous, largely unspecified resources (simplistically finance) that are handed down from some higher often anonymous authority, usually personified under the designation of 'government' or 'the council'. This means that most of us seek and are recipients of 'help' rather than 'power'.

The professional ego-state as the 'giver' of power (help) appears to prevent a rational understanding that power, in every day life in our society, is the use of influence to gain authority and that authority can only be 'taken'; authority is activating control – control, in the first instance over ourselves in society. Someone else cannot give me control over myself, although they can and do attempt to prevent this by exerting authority over me, part of which is convincing me that I need empowerment by way of some professional activity (help/support).

Without that professional intervention I am seen as necessarily to remain relatively powerless. But even when I am notionally given power, it is not power because I have no idea what 'power' means in this context. Having been defined by the professional I am unable to articulate my own situation and as such I am in no position to realise or use my influence to take authority. The professional incursion (intervention) has placed me in a maze of confusing terminology that they, like the latter day priestly class they replaced, are relied upon to interpret. The client then dances to the professional's tune that is played from the score of organisational and state policy. The ironic symmetry of the procedure is almost poetic.

The importance of media companies.

Media companies exist to sell a product to a market; that is all – they have no other social or benevolent purpose. We now have an economy that is internationalised; the global economy as it is called (globalisation). We have become more conscious over the last few years that vast sums of unregulated financial capital circulate around the world largely untracked. At the same time commodities (sugar, copper, pork for instance) are bought and sold that do not actually exist. A company in the USA has made a fortune selling rights to property on the moon where no such rights exist. As we have seen over the last few years this now overwhelms the most powerful of economies and countries; no nation could do much to address the credit crunch; it even seems beyond control of great collectives of national economies. European States and the United States combined could not defend their economies against the whims of financial capital – no one really had much of an idea of what was happening until it had happened, and when it did happen no one had any concrete notion of what to do about it. Extraordinary amounts of money had been supposedly lost, but it could not be made totally clear to whom it had been lost to. It had just 'gone' probably because it never existed in any corporal sense – money (like community and informality) is a notional, conceptual phenomenon.

Sales of international corporations have been greater than all of world trade for decades and what is known as world trade is really a bit of a joke. Most of what is called 'trade' is internal transfers within a handful of particular corporations. Centrally managed interchanges are made openly and those institutions generate their own interests and that is what they are interested in, not the interests of employees, poorer countries, the environment, communities or young people; they exist to perpetuate themselves – nothing else. Whatever they do is geared, *has* to be geared, not to profit, but to their own constant growth. This again is no secret. It doesn't matter if a company's profit is a billion dollars, it is seen as a disaster if these profits fall by three per cent. This is plastered all over the financial pages of every newspaper in the world and is bleated at us through the internet, on television and radio; it is not a clandestine plot, it's blatant and in your face. Connections between big corporations and the state are not covert: every time you buy anything reliant on oil, petrol, plastic, fabrics, you are paying directly into the US exchequer: all oil is traded in American dollars.

As the media conglomerates have become internationalised they have developed some of the same interests and they have set up their own governing institutions. The World Bank, the IMF, GATT and the G7 Executive and so on are in effect a kind of world government that more or less look after the interests of multi-national corporations and international financial interests. They might express concern about poverty but this is because a certain level of poverty within particular geographical areas is not good for their interests. There is no concern per se about starvation or illiteracy. Again these words have one meaning to you and me but in the lexicon of capitalism they have other economic meanings and according to their context they mean either 'gain' or 'loss' for financial interests – no more.

The media, which include the dominant publishing houses and newspapers, as well as the internet and television and now the mobile phone industry, is a part of this, and we only get told what we need to know, or more realistically what a relatively few people at the head of multinational corporations want us to know (via the media they control). At the moment you can read this book because a small number of independent publishing houses are still around that do not see it as against their interest to publish it. But another reason exists for this book being published by the publisher it is published by. The publisher of this book has an enduring commitment to critical analysis, the search for truth and open argument. It is not part of a multinational corporation that would be contradicting its own logic by publishing it. How long this will be possible is anybody's guess. As long as people are interested or curious about things I suppose; as long as people feel compelled to question?

For all this, what the young people we deal with watch, hear and read is controlled, in the main, by these great corporate interests – the multi-national media and by association the transnational corporations. These entities do not have the human interests of young people at heart. This is the huge and perhaps sometimes seemingly overwhelming problem youth workers have to face; MTV, Facebook, mobile phone culture and MySpace are individually much more influential than all the youth workers in the country combined. And then some. As soon as we get our heads around that, and get out of the professional ego-state of seeing ourselves as 'givers of power' and/or 'educators of communities', the better. These fantasies that we have been seduced into by state sanctioned and controlled training agencies and literature brought forth by the publishing arms of multi-national corporations are in practice making us less effective because we are operating in and abetting the continuation of a dream state of practice. There are some clues that slip though the net about such things. Morpheus (ibid) provides a commentary on this 'dream state':

The Matrix is a system ... when you're inside, you look around, what do you see? Businessmen, teachers, lawyers, carpenters. The very minds of the people we are trying to save. But until we do, these people are still a part of that system ... You have to understand, most of these people are not ready to be unplugged. And many of them are so inured, so hopelessly dependent on the system, that they will fight to protect it.

My guess is many angry readers of this book will fight to protect/justify the 'system'. But none of this is new. The energy companies have long been international concerns and have for that time been instruments of American foreign policy. This is why it was important for international capital to denationalise British energy interests. We were seduced into buying shares in what already belonged to us on the promises of huge profits for all; but of course it never happened. The public bought the shares and most sold them pretty quickly as soon as the prices were artificially inflated to facilitate this, gaining about a ten per cent return on their investment overall. This is nothing to what has been made on the same shares since by multinational concerns. But now the scale is quite different to what it was even 20 years ago. These large firms have a huge amount of control over the domestic policy of the United States and the other big economies. Governments have to ask what that $50 trillion of financial capital is going to do if they do X, Y and Z. President Obama has decided to stimulate the economy and now he's got to count on the fact that they'll be a reduction in the sales of treasury securities and government bonds, which means the interest rates will go up, which means such and such impact on the economy. That terminates action. This illustrates how terribly limited governments are. This just leaves individual action to address injustice, poverty and so on. What I, Chomsky and Illich are saying is that you just can't rely on anything else and this is authoritative information for young people.

This huge financial capital that has been floating around the globe has had an anti-growth effect. It has driven countries to special kinds of policies, deflationary, low growth, low wage economies. This has affected foreign policy too. It's a very serious constraint. If the international investing community or big corporations don't like some foreign policy initiative they can act in various subtle ways to make the conditions on it hard. This is one of the central reasons why tax payers all over the world have had to bail out banks. The nexus is so tightly drawn between the state and globalised capital that whole countries and continents are webbed up in the concerns of international finance.

At the time of writing there seems a focus of this type on China. While China is the first port of call in terms of national borrowing (to support Western financial institutions) it relies on those it is supporting financially to buy its goods. As it lends more to keep its markets alive at the same time the price of its products fall – this is a corrosive situation in terms of China's social structure – but maybe that is no accident? As unemployment grows in China so does social unrest. As such the future of China is in the hands of international capitalism and what it might want China to be.

Again this is not really something totally new. In 1968 for example, after the Tet offensive in Vietnam, US corporations basically decided that the war was getting too costly, so they essentially gave the orders to the US government, instructing Linden Johnson to start negotiations. Now the phenomenon is considerably greater. Nixon broke down the post war economic system and this set in motion all sorts of things, like transnationalisation of the American economy, which effected everything that governments can do.

America unchallenged

The effect of the breakdown of superpower rivalry was entirely predicable. The Soviet Union was a deterrent to US actions and to some extent this worked in reverse, although the relationship between American and the USSR was never a balanced one – the USA was always far more powerful than the Soviet Union, and both sides understood that. It is true that the USSR internally was much more brutal, externally it was more conservative than the Americans. The USA was a global power, Soviet interventions were limited to its borders; the 'interventions' (yes, like youth workers they 'intervene' – another word with at least two meanings) of the US were and are evident everywhere. But the existence of a relatively powerful deterrent certainly restricted US foreign policy. As the USSR declined it was recognised by America that it would be more at liberty to intervene anywhere it wanted as there would no longer be an automatic effect from its long time rival. Intervention required new pretexts. Between 1917 and 1989 there was a spontaneous effect. The US wanted to invade a country and to do so simply meant pointing to the 'Communist threat'. Prior to 1917 the British or the Germans were the threats. After 1989 another excuse had to be found. Now of course it is Islam.

George Bush senior, after the fall of the Berlin wall, which effectively ended the Cold War, invaded Panama. America installed a small rich clique of Bankers and narcotic dealers who would do what they were told by the US government. This is not historically exceptional action by the US but two things about it were novel. It was the first time in around 70 years that America invaded a country other than ostensibly to 'Stop the Russians'. A month after the Berlin wall fell it would have been hard to use that justification. So, the invasion was justified as an action that was defending America against Hispanic narcotic traffickers lead by the Panamanian President Manuel Noriega, although he had been defined as a US ally up to only a couple of years before the invasion. The American President's Latin American specialists openly pointed out that this was the first time that the USA had been able to 'intervene' without the worry of counter action anywhere by the USSR.

The next big intervention was the first Gulf war and as many commentators pointed out the traditional warrior states the US and the UK, the enforcers, 10 years earlier would not have presumed to put half a million personnel in the desert as it would have been much too dangerous in terms of world peace. This time they could do anything they wanted. And did. Arbitrary force was used against a comparatively defenceless non-industrialised power. Yes Iraq had the fourth biggest army in the world, but as the legendary American stand-up comedian, the late Bill Hicks, pointed out, 'there's a mighty big difference between the world's third biggest army and the fourth'. At the same time there is a big difference between the world's forth biggest army and the world's most powerful military machine. It is intriguing to note that immediately prior to the build-up to the invasion of Iraq that oil rich nation had ceased to trade oil in dollars in favour of Euros.

The role of US and Western force was to make the world safe for the multi-nationals to operate in (in the words of Billy Bragg, 'We're making the world safe for capitalism'). This creates the industrial/technological environment that Illich talks about, the environment that alienates the young people we work with.

The main economic weekly in India some years ago described the economic plans of the Indian government. India is not Nicaragua; it is a big, fast developing nation. The writer declared that it was pointless to look at the Indian government plans because they were just coming straight from the World Bank, and therefore Washington (and vice-versa). Furthermore, the Indian press has pointed out that the wording, even the spelling, used in Indian national planning is now American rather than English and in a style that would be natural to an Indian Bureaucrat. That's because the policy emanates from Washington. American power is so enormous. It is exercised through what are, in part, its agencies, like the IMF and the World Bank (collective incarnations of the multinationals). Even a huge country like India is not only given its directions, but it is even given them in the words and spelling that come out of Washington. Science is done in English and that's nothing to do with English but its got everything to do with US power.

This is important to know because our policies for young people have their root in multi-national interests rather than the 'good' of youth. But as Morpheus tells us, *There is a difference between knowing the path and walking the path.* Knowing makes the walking a different experience as we then journey in consciousness rather than sleepwalking. Instead of pursuing an illusion that we are travelling of our own free will to a destination we have decided on, which will ultimately prove false and as such disappointing and moral sapping, we can begin to understand what is pushing us and where we are being channelled towards. This makes authentic resistance possible. And that is probably as 'free' as it gets in our society.

Britain does not have an equal relationship with America. Anglo-American culture does not exist. The UK has an illusion that a 'special relationship' with the US exists, but this is laughable. This was recently made clear when newly elected President Obama returned a bust of Churchill that been sitting in the White House when he moved in. Publicly American leaders make out that Britain and America are buddies, but confidentially they say something different. The declassified internal records show influential advisors to President Kennedy calling the UK 'our lieutenant'. This does not suggest a 'partnership' so much as 'bultlership'. Europe is much more under US cultural domination now than it has been at any time in history outside of post-World-War years. European newspapers look evermore like the New York Times or the Washington Post. We are colonised. In Britain the subordination to US power is mind boggling.

This has not peaked. Yes, Spanish will soon be the most commonly spoken first language in the industrialised world and the Far East has economically been in ascendancy, but it is the poor who speak Spanish and it is not the intention of those with authority that they will have much of an influence on the future. The international language of China, India and Japan is English, American-English. Japan and its former colonies, its economic periphery, are culturally speaking, to a large extent, under US influence. Students from that part of the world look to go to America to study. Half the classes in many US universities are made up of students from the Far-East. In the long term the East may become an independent force (although this has never been allowed to the Arabs, who share culture, religion and language) but the US is more influential now in the Far East than it was 20 or 30 years ago.

What can be said?

It is those with authority to control who determine what can be said by the exploited. While the wise do not speak their mind so that order will not turn to chaos. The famous Chicago school, well known in the world of sociology (before it became dominated by ideological fanatics), pointed out that freedom without power, just like power without freedom, is intolerable. Those we work for and among have freedom of a sort, but authority? How do we create environments wherein power can be realised in the taking of authority, given the situation I have described with the help of Chomsky and Illich?

It is crucially important to defend freedom of speech. The US and the UK are still the most likely places that you will be allowed to say what you like, although who will be able to hear is questionable, as this is controlled by the media. But the US and UK are capitalist countries. In this situation everything is a commodity. Freedom is a commodity. You get about as much as you can buy. Perhaps the middle class citizen (they really are citizens in the US, we are not citizens in the UK, we are subjects of Her Majesty the Queen. This means that constitutionally we have no rights as understood in a republic like the US – there are only duties and laws in Britain), has quite a deal of free speech. The poor black living in New Orleans or Lewisham really has no freedom of speech merely because they can say what they like; saying what you like is not difficult, being heard presents the problems. This situation is made worse when you really have no idea what is going on; all you know is what the media tell you . . . what the state *wants* you to know.

Chomsky is in a position to understand this. One of his first books on the media was published by a flourishing publisher, but the publisher was owned by the huge multi-national, Warner Communications (Bugs Bunny and all that). And it didn't like the book. So it put the publisher out of business. Not just Chomsky's book was wiped out; every book the publisher published was destroyed. This tells us something about the books that get published and their writers. What's up Doc.? That latent power has enormous effect on what actually happens, and in the media it is just as overwhelming. While there is no official ban on Chomsky, he is hardly ever heard on television or radio compared say to Jerry Springer, Jeremy Kyle or Boris Johnson.

Western culture is shot through by a profoundly totalitarian force. Critical and dissenting voices are excluded, not by an official ban, but various informal (another word we know to have two meanings) devices. We hear an awful lot from the media about global warming, but very little of the counter argument – what does this tell us?

This totalitarian streak is not unrelated to the fact that we live in a relatively free society. One thing that has been recognised, even in the academic realm, is that the more free a society, the more you must control opinion. If you can control people with a bludgeon, you don't care much what they think. If you can't control people with a bludgeon, you'd better control what they think (see Foucault 1977) because they might give you trouble. So in the Soviet Union about 75 per cent of the population listened to foreign radio broadcasts, and about half the population read underground publications.

In Britain and the US no one listens to foreign broadcasts, the dissident press reaches hardly anyone. You listen, watch and read the 'right' things. You march out into the 'community' because you have been told it is there (even though no one can quite say what or where it is) and undertake 'informal education' with this indistinct entity. All these words, phrases and intents have more than one meaning but often we only understand the one we have been told by organisations or media that have an interest in telling you what they want you to know. So you and those you work with are pacified. But there is some transparency if you look for it. On 28 August 2009 James (son of Rupert) Murdoch, chair and chief executive of News Corp, Europe and Asia, in the MacTaggart lecture told the world that 'profit is the only guarantor of independence' in the media while a few days later (1 September) London mayor said on BBC Radio Five Live that society needed to 'support and guarantee' the City of London and its activities – so much for 'free markets' – we should only know that which makes a profit while we should allow financial speculators a consequence free life as we punish young people for down-loading a James Brown rift!

What to do?

The media and the intellectual community are keen to keep the gates tightly closed. This is because of the danger of letting people in a free society think. According to Illich, this increasing disempowerment of people needs to be addressed. A new form of social relations is possible, based on the enlargement of each person's competence, control and initiative. This is only limited by the claims of other individuals to an equal range of power (authority) and freedom. Technology should be used to serve interrelated individuals – this is what Illich thinks of as 'conviviality'.

This must involve an aim for 'austerity', using the meaning first put forward by Thomas Aquinas – we need to develop our capacities for disciplined and creative playfulness. This does not exclude enjoyment but it does mean looking to minimalise activity that distracts from or is destructive of personal relatedness, which is a complementary part of a more embracing virtue, friendship and joyfulness. Things or tools could destroy rather than enhance 'eutrapelia', graceful playfulness, in personal relations.

What Chomsky and Illich seem to imply is that we can start with basic relations. The mechanics and principles of 'macro-systems' are so corrupted and distorted that it is a waste of time to look to them for the betterment of the human condition. Eutrapelia and forms of 'austerity' can form the basis of a liberation attitude and a process of conviviality. This is the beginning and foundation of an alternative social formation. In a sense it is all we have. Both our glory and our poverty is that all we have is ourselves. There is no Justice, just us!

The way of the guerrilla

Seventeen days after I watched Celtic and Racing club in Montevideo (see above) with the assistance of the CIA, Argentinean revolutionary Che Guevara was murdered in one of Uruguay's northern neighbours, Bolivia. Che's theories of guerrilla warfare instructed that the guerrilla group can dedicate itself exclusively to running away from an encirclement, which is the enemy's only way of obliging the band into a decisive fight that could be unfavourable. The guerrillas can also change the battle into a counter-encirclement. Guevara described this as a kind of dance (minuet): the guerrilla bands encircle an enemy position completely from the four points of the compass, with a few fighters in each place, far enough away to avoid being encircled themselves; the battle is started by the guerrillas at any one of these points, this draws the opposing army towards one of the guerrilla groups. But the guerrillas retreat, always maintaining visual contact, however as one group retire another initiates an attack from a different point. The army will repeat its action and the guerrillas respond in the same way. Thus the enemy is immobilised, forcing it to expend large quantities of ammunition and weakening the morale of its troops while the guerrillas avoid any great danger. These tactics were deployed in Vietnam, South Africa and are being deployed in Iraq and Afghanistan.

I have always thought of youth work as a 'guerrilla' profession; the word is derived from the Spanish, 'little war' and youth workers tend to be involved in little wars. We are generally deployed in small bands and our work can draw attention if we are effective but to continue this other bands have to be doing something of the same thing. This is what allows our work to endure to cultivate conviviality.

Against the rigidity of classical methods of fighting, the guerrilla fighter invents their own tactics at every minute of the fight and constantly surprises the enemy. This, in the practice context, might be thought of as the honing of professional judgement.

For Che, the enemy, after easily overcoming difficulties in a gradual advance, is often surprised to find itself suddenly and solidly detained, the possibility of moving forward prevented (this has happened in both Iraq and Afghanistan). This is because the guerrilla-defended positions, when they have been selected after careful study of the ground, are invulnerable. It is not the number of attacking soldiers that makes the difference, but the number of defending soldiers. Once that number has been placed it can nearly always hold off a battalion with success. But it is crucial to choose well the moment and the place for defending a position without retreat.

The guerrilla way of attacking is also different; beginning with surprise and fury. Irresistible, it suddenly changes into total passivity. The surviving enemy believes that the attack is over and starts to relax, to return to a routine, when suddenly a new attack bursts forth in another place with the same characteristics, while the main body of the guerrilla band lies in wait to intercept reinforcements. At other times an outpost defending the camp will be suddenly attacked by guerrillas, dominated, and captured. The fundamental thing is surprise and rapidity of attack.

Acts of sabotage are very important. 'Sabotage' is a term borrowed from French syndicalists by American labour organisations at the turn of the 20th century. It means the hampering of productivity and efficiency. In terms of youth work, this might be understood as assisting individuals, groups and communities in examining and questioning decisions that effect them rather than just accepting direct implementation. This may feel demoralising for authority figures who have a vested interest in enacting their wishes without the inclusion ('interference') of those directly effected by the same. However, what is experienced as 'demoralising' for one group is often 'morale enhancing' for others.

Informing the likes of local authorities, pressure and rights groups, certain parts of the local media, mayoral offices, councillors, MPs and MEPs, of wide constituent disapproval, via alternative arguments for – or against – proposed commercial or State incursions into a neighbourhood, for example, negatively affects the direct and unmediated communication particular interests might otherwise have enjoyed with these guardians of the public interest and conduits of authority.

It is necessary to distinguish clearly between sabotage, a highly effective method of warfare, and terrorism, a measure that is generally ineffective and indiscriminate. No youth worker should ever defy their job description or foul policy – this only marks them out as a guerrilla target. According to Guevara, to be effective the guerrilla (youth worker) needs to learn how to pick up the enemy's weapons and use these resources against them. Choose the ground that you want to fight on but, above all, live to fight another day.

In the end Celtic lost in Montevideo. If ever you have occasion to study the match (see Belton, 2008) you will perhaps detect that it was Racing Club that, consciously or not, who deployed what might be understood as guerrilla tactics, which involved acts of sabotage, while in confusion, Celtic were condemned to answer with ineffective acts of terrorism.

References

Belton, B. (2008) *The Battle of Montevideo*. History Press.

Chomsky, N. (1998) *Propaganda and Control of the Public Mind*. An audio CD recording of the Harvard Trade Union Program by Noam Chomsky. Alternative Tentacle.

Chomsky, N. (2000) *Chomsky on Miseducation*. Rowman and Littlefield.

Chomsky, N. (2009) *Manufacturing Consent: Noam Chomsky and the Media*. Bfi DVD.

Fairclough, F. (1985) *Critical Discourse Analysis*. Longman.

Foucault, M. (1977) *Discipline and Punish: Birth of the Prison*. Viking.

Guevara, C. (1985) *Guerilla Warfare*. University Nebraska Press.
Illich, I. (1971) *Deschooling Society.* Harper Collins.
Illich, I. (1973) *Tools for Conviviality.*
Illich, I. (1977) *Disabling Professions.* Marion Boyars Publishers Ltd.
Irwin, W. (Ed.) (2002) *The 'Matrix' and Philosophy: Welcome to the Desert of the Real.* Open Court.
Laswell, H.D. (1905) *The World Revolution of Our Time: A Framework for Basic Policy Research.* University Press.
Maxwell, J. (2000) *Matrix of Power: How the World Has Been Controlled by Powerful People Without Your Knowledge.* Tree.
Wachowski, A. and Wachowski, L. (1999) *The Matrix*.
Wachowski, A. and Wachowski, L. (2003) *The Matrix Reloaded*.
Wachowski, A. and Wachowski, L. (2003) *The Matrix Revolutions*.

7

Taking Sides: Dilemmas and Possibilities for 'Radical' Youth Work

Taking Sides explores the potential of engendering radical youth work theory, looking at what might be considered as foundation literature and possible future developments. As such, it necessarily adopts more of an academic approach than other chapters of this book.

The chapter has been adapted from an original paper written by Tania de St Croix. Moving from an effort to stimulate theory building by way of an emphasis on practice critique and the honing of professional judgement, Tania shifts the perspective of the book, tightening the focus on the trajectory of literature that specifically uses the practice realm as a focal point.

Tania has been involved in youth work, play schemes and community activism since leaving school in 1993. She grew up in Bath and has mostly lived and worked there and in Manchester. She is currently a detached youth worker for a small charity in Hackney, London.

I would like to thank her for her important contribution to this book.

As youth work is increasingly subsumed within the capitalist project, professionals in the field are finding it difficult to claim political neutrality without demonstrating a professional death wish. This chapter examines whether there is a 'radical' form of youth work which takes sides against the growing incursion of capitalist influence on practice, consequent authoritarian attitudes extended to practitioners and young people alike and ecological destruction.

A definition of radical youth work is proposed which emphasises resistance and a political perspective as well as methodological values. Using this definition, I will review radical influences on youth work debates and practice. The concept of radical youth work challenges those of us involved in the field to choose to analyse the situation efficiently and effectively; if we fail to do this, youth work will become more firmly entrenched as a form of social control. We have for a long time been walking in our sleep, hoping for the best as a profession. This has resulted in the undermining of our professional credibility.

In search of niches and forgotten corners

My motivation for writing this chapter is to make some sense of the contradictions and possibilities of trying to live out ecological and anarchist beliefs while attempting to be a 'good' youth worker. A brief personal history: I left school full of naïve political vigour, fresh from fighting the school mock election as a Green Party candidate and interested in neither university nor career. I worked as a volunteer with a play scheme and a youth project and went to live on a local anti-road action camp. A year later, the road protest fizzled out and I got my first paid play-work job. I began to experience something of a dual identity as public services worker and political activist. Challenges included negotiating the clash between professional and activist cultures, explaining my criminal convictions to employers, and managing my time and energy between two demanding and unpredictable activities. In recent years I have prioritised my youth worker identity, while trying to maintain at least some political integrity.

This has not always been successful. My condescending vision of raising the consciousness of young people was obstructed by the everyday realities of youth work, especially because I had no coherent theory to support my practice. I will attempt to address the latter at least and hope this exercise will be helpful to others. When I began reading I was struck by two things. First, despite many youth workers identifying themselves as anti-authoritarian, surprisingly little is written on the subject of youth work resisting the status quo, especially when compared with the more extensive literature on radical schooling (see Wright, 1989 and Hicks, 2004 for useful overviews on radical education). I realised I could not investigate radical youth work before asking whether such a concept even exists. Second, I discovered a widely held view that youth work's survival is threatened (e.g. Davies, 2006; Jeffs, 2002; Jeffs and Smith, 2006; Tiffany, 2007). This perceived threat to youth work is part of the backdrop to the motivation for what follows.

In their critique of government youth policy, Jeffs and Smith (2006: 36) argue:

> *For youth work to survive with any integrity it will be necessary to exploit niches and forgotten corners; and to hide from, or at least stay out of sight of, key State surveillance systems.*

I am won over by this hint at youth work practice which is prepared to duck state surveillance to preserve its integrity. The search for 'niches and forgotten corners' suggested the questions I have attempted to tackle. However the problem with 'hiding' is, as Botteheim (1979) argues, that it is a limited tactic (as evidenced by the case of Anne Frank). But can I justify approaching youth work from a political perspective? Is a notion of 'radical youth work' meaningful, and if so, how can it be defined? Is there a history of radical youth work? How do youth workers from radical perspectives experience the dilemmas and contradictions of working 'in and against the state' (London-Edinburgh Weekend Return Group 1980)? What are the possibilities, if any, for future radical youth work theory and practice?

Youth work lacks an extensive literature (Gilchrist et al., 2003). There is little recent writing from an explicitly anti-capitalist (but see Taylor, 1987, 2000, 2007) or ecological perspectives on youth work. By and large the literature tends towards liberal reformism (e.g. Francique, 2007) not really assessing the role of the state in any significant depth. Much of this material apparently takes the view that the provision of youth work is made for mostly benign reasons. This can only be named as naive and I hope my arguments can strengthen youth work theory, connecting it more firmly to wider social and political considerations. I also hope that it stimulates debate and adds meaning to my own youth work practice. As Karl Marx (1845) argued, 'The philosophers have only interpreted the world in various ways; the point, however, is to change it'. I hope, at least, to change my own actions in the world by developing a more coherent and contextual theoretical understanding. Ideally, I hope what I have to say will spark thoughts, agreements and disagreements amongst others interested in whether there is or can be such a phenomenon that might be understood as radical youth work.

My approach is influenced by values developed partly through my experience of reading, talking and thinking about 'radical youth work', which has challenged my values. It therefore seemed natural to me to at points use narrative forms to 'tell my tale'. The possibilities of educational research as narrative are explored by writers such as Clough (2002) and Richardson (1990, 1996). In this chapter, my interest in storytelling is simply its potential to bring coherence to seemingly chaotic processes. In this I have been inspired by Wells (1986: xii) who argues 'The available evidence is given meaning by being embedded in a story in which it makes sense'. I need to show my 'working out' as if in a GCSE maths paper. Wells (1986: xiii) again makes a valuable argument:

> *The evidence is never so complete or so unambiguous as to rule out alternative interpretations. The important criteria in judging the worth of a story are: does it fit the facts as I have observed them and does it provide a helpful basis for future action?*

The approach of Clough and Nutbrown (2002: 10) both attracts and dismays me. I support their argument that researchers have their own perspective, and that:

> *. . . research which did not express a more or less distinct perspective on the world would not be research at all; it would have the status of a telephone directory where data are listed without analysis.*

Clough and Nutbrown (2002: 38) seem undecided whether methodology is instrumental or value-based. Something of their worldview is suggested by their argument that:

> *In the end, the characteristic task of a methodology is to persuade the reader of the **unavoidably** triangular connection between these research questions, **these** methods used to operationalise them and **these** data so generated* (emphasis in original).

I oppose this linear view of inquiry, and am suspicious of social research methodologies which claim to be scientific and factual. As Altrichter (1993: 43) argues, a connection exists between educational research and professionalism which 'cannot be conceived as instrumental problem-solving, because the 'problem' is usually not unambiguously given'. Here I present my methods in the knowledge that I could have chosen different methodological options and that my findings are far from being inevitable because, 'the future is problematic and not already decided, fatalistically' (Freire, 1998: 26). This does not mean I believe 'anything goes', and I aim to be coherent and 'build on (my) intentions and submit them to method and rigorous analysis' (Freire, 1998: 48).

Although limited by youth work's low profile in print generally, I have grown aware of many key debates in the field, but needing to find a focus, Paulo Freire's theories on reading became inspirational:

We should not submit to the text or be submissive in front of the text. The thing is to fight with the text, even though loving it.

Freire and Shor, 1987: 11

My political motivations are highly relevant to the subject matter of this piece and I agree with Fairclough (2001: 4) that:

. . . it is important not only to acknowledge these influences rather than affecting a spurious neutrality about social issues, but also to be open with one's readers about where one stands.

The affiliations with which I initially approached this research are presented above, and I attempt to be clear about my own beliefs, assumptions and arguments throughout the chapter.

But as indicated above, my primary influence is Freire (1988, 1998) the Marxist-influenced Brazilian activist and educator who argues that students should be actively engaged in learning which arises from their own experience. I did not approach what follows as an empty vessel in search of pure knowledge, but as a committed youth worker with twelve years experience, aiming to develop 'critical capacity, curiosity and rigour' (Freire, 1998: 33). Throughout, I aim to make theoretical and human connections and to develop strategies to deal with the contradictions between my identities as an anarchist and a youth worker. Beyond the individual level I hope to spark criticism, thoughtfulness and debate around the possibilities and problems of radical youth work.

In structure the chapter moves broadly from the general to the specific. The first section sets the context, arguing that youth work is affected by ideology and can never be a neutral endeavour. In the second section I develop a theory and definition of radical youth work. Section three looks for radical influences on ideological struggle in the history of modern youth work, while the fourth section focuses on attempts at radical practice. In this context, section five reflects on some of my own experiences of dilemmas in radical youth work. In the conclusion I summarise the key dilemmas and possibilities of radical youth work.

But what is clear is that we cannot hide forever – that is the way of the ineffectual convictional coward rather than a means of purposeful activism.

The myth of the neutral youth worker

I once believed youth work meant working alongside young people for positive change. Others define youth work as 'giving kids something to do', 'building relationships' or 'social and political education'. These different language choices inevitably reflect different ideological positions (Fairclough, 1995). The background to this chapter, then, is not a neutral description of what youth work is. Instead I argue that everything that is said, written or done about youth work is affected by ideologies. I am aware that those of us on the political left inevitably fill our writing with the questioning of commonsense, the problematising of concepts, the dissecting of language. This tendency put me off reading theory as a novice youth worker. I used to think, 'why do we have to question everything? Get to the point!' But youth work is a product of struggle, debate and competing ideologies, and if youth workers don't try to understand this then we'll probably support the existing political system by default perhaps without even realising it.

Ideology is what people believe to be common sense, or in Meighan and Siraj-Blatchford's (2003: 186) words:

> . . . a broad interlocked set of ideas and beliefs about the world held by a group of people that they demonstrate in both behaviour and conversation to various audiences . . . they become the taken-for-granted way of making sense of the world.

Youth work has professional ideologies, often formalised as 'good practice' guidelines. It is also shaped by the varied ideologies of its work force, its young participants and the wider structures in which it operates. This challenges the idea that it is possible to be a politically neutral youth worker. For Freire (1998: 90) so-called neutral education:

> . . . uses the classroom to inculcate in the students political attitudes and practices, as if it were possible to exist as a human being in the world and at the same time be neutral.

Shaw (2003: 229) argues that in community work 'neutrality is not an option, for 'no politics' inevitably means "their politics"'. Similarly, youth work that does not actively support social change inevitably supports the status quo.

Fairclough (1995: 34) argues, 'Alternative lexicalisations are generated from divergent ideological positions'. These may be conscious or unconscious, as a brief critical analysis of my earlier youth work definition demonstrates. 'Working alongside' suggests equality between young people and adults in the youth work relationship. But hierarchy is rarely absent in reality, and my phrasing is rather utopian. 'Young people' is professional youth work jargon which indicates 'young people perceived and received as young people rather than . . . through the filter of adult-imposed labels' (Davies 2005: 11). Just as social workers refer to 'clients' and teachers to 'pupils', the phrase 'young people' is also adult-imposed, but intends to show respect. The phrase 'young people' also assumes a commonly understood and socially constructed stage of life between childhood and adulthood. 'Positive change' implies my opposition to the status quo, but its unqualified use assumes a common understanding of good and bad and a pluralist belief in change generally. As Thomas (1978: 240) argues, 'the plain, but uninteresting, fact is that most human transactions can be conceptualised as change activities'. My definition reflected some of my beliefs but was rather naïve and vague.

Lack of theory makes youth workers particularly susceptible to such vagueness. Jeffs and Smith (2003: 75) argue that the weaknesses of youth work arise from:

> . . . the extent to which workers fail to rise above the 'taken for granted', and are unable to develop the sort of sophisticated ways of working that are necessary.

There are at least three reasons for this. First, youth work's low status leads to workers prioritising survival over analysis; criticism risks projects and jobs and can therefore be seen as disloyal. Second, the growing culture of public service managerialism promotes the myth that workers have commonly agreed goals and need only find out how best to achieve them. Third, there is a common tendency of resistance to theory. The following quote from a playleader is typical of this anti-intellectual discourse:

> Frankly I believe that academic degrees are of no help in this field of work; it is some other elusive quality which ensures that a playground always seems to be a hive of activity.

Lambert and Pearson 1974: 20

There has always been a somewhat tenuous relationship between youth work ideology and what actually happens in youth clubs and projects, leading to suggestions that the practice of youth work tends to be more conservative than its liberal theory (Leigh and Smart, 1985; Taylor, 1987). This divide between ideas and practice is partly related to youth work itself, which must focus its practice on what young people want or they will leave. This is why, for example, a youth worker may aim to work for social change but spend much of her time organising pool tournaments and bowling trips. Another factor limiting the practice of progressive theories is the ongoing attack on left wing movements generally. Many socialist youth workers are disillusioned or exhausted after experiencing the defeat of the old labour movement, symbolised by the demise of the great miners' strike (Taylor, 2007).

Lack of theory has led to 'an interesting myth about the lack of coherence to youth work practice' (Leigh and Smart, 1985: 21). Before going on to define radical youth work specifically it is therefore important to identify what is fundamental and distinctive about youth work generally. Davies (2005) and Jeffs and Smith (2003) have written in more depth on this subject, but for the purposes of this paper I argue that youth work's distinctiveness can be summarised in three features:

1. A social education purpose.
2. Informal methods.
3. The principle of voluntary participation (young people choosing whether to take part).

These features are repeatedly emphasised across different ideologies and types of youth work (e.g. DfES, 2002; Jeffs, 2002; Jeffs and Smith, 2006; Nicholls, 2005; Robertson, 2001; Spence et al., 2003; Tiffany, 2007; Williams, 1988; Wylie, 2001; Young, 1999).

Youth work is influenced by ideology in the language used to describe it, the features which define it and what takes place under its name. Where consensus exists, it results from ideological struggle by workers, young people and others. Youth work's social educational purpose was established during its professionalisation in the late 1930s (Smith, 2001) and has been defended since then (Jeffs and Smith, 1994, 2006). The informal approach survives so far, despite attacks by government-imposed curricula, inspection and bureaucracy (Davies, 1986; Harris, 2005; Jeffs, 1997; Stanton, 2004; Tiffany, 2007). The principle of voluntary participation remains despite pressure to target and monitor supposedly 'problematic' individuals (Bradford, 1997; Jeffs and Smith, 1994; Jeffs and Smith, 2006). These key features of youth work have endured for nearly 70 years despite attempts by the political right to undermine them.

Towards a theory of 'radical' youth work

What is 'radical youth work'? Some time ago my radical youth worker identity was a matter of instinct and I had no clear answer to this question, so I found myself searching for a theory of radical youth work, but while the concept existed in youth work literature (e.g. Bradford, 1997; Butters and Newall, 1978; Leigh and Smart, 1985) it was rarely theorised in detail. I needed a definition or framework of radical youth work but one based on my own experience and informed by theory. Although youth work lacks extensive written theory, 'people routinely use theories without making them explicit or labelling them as such' (Bond, 2004: 13). Youth work theory tends to be grounded in practical experience, often containing inadequately considered assumptions (Flowers, 1998). To develop a theory of radical youth work I initially considered some of my own assumptions.

My choice of the word 'radical' requires justification because it is rooted in my (sub-) cultural context. I identify as a radical because of my history and continuing identification with environmental and anti-capitalist direct action movements. I take my political identity into my workplace, both inevitably and intentionally. I use my skills, and try to provide spaces, to enable young people to practice co-operative community; I aim to be a political educator, but a questioning influence rather than a propagandist; and I believe in young people taking authority for themselves, using it to care for others and the planet as well as themselves. Specifically I call myself an ecological anarchist but, while I make no secret of this, there are probably few ecological anarchist youth workers. In this chapter therefore I am interested in a broader category of political conviction which I sum up with the word 'radical'.

In common usage the word 'radical' suggests extremity on any political spectrum, for example, 'Thatcher's radical welfare reforms', 'radical Islamists' and 'radical animal rights activists'. The less political use implies newness, as in 'The BBC today unveiled radical plans to rebuild its website' (*Guardian*, 2006), a usage which paradoxically results from radical's older meaning as 'returning to the roots'. However, the political sub-cultural meaning of 'radical' is also valid. Building a political movement includes creating or changing language, and the word radical is used by left-wing and anarchist movements. These encompass people who label themselves as anarchists, socialists, communists, feminists, anti-racists, environmentalists, those who identify with various labels, and those who avoid political labels. As many differences exist within each group as between them, so the catch-all 'radical' is usefully vague. It is used by professional groups including teachers, social workers, community workers and midwives, but is harder to find in youth work theory.

Tony Jeffs wrote an article entitled, 'Whatever happened to radical youth work?' (2002: 4). Jeffs presents youth work history as dominated by two ideological traditions, conservative and radical, with the latter in decline. His concept of radical youth work is most clearly articulated in this passage:

> *There has always been a radical tradition within youth work, of workers committed to not merely working with young people, but working with young people in order to try and create a better society. Something that is about radical root and branch reform.*

But if radical youth work is about creating a better society, what would this society look like? This question is barely addressed. While agreeing with Jeffs' analysis that there are different ideological traditions in youth work, I would argue that to reduce them to two traditions is overly simplistic and leads to a broad definition which encompasses socialist, liberal and all non-conservative youth work. A narrower definition would usefully distinguish radical youth work from reformist liberalism.

Canadian academic Hans Skott-Myhre (2005, 2006) conceptualises radical youth work from a specifically Marxist perspective. In a recent article with Gretzinger (undated) he defines radical youth work as:

> *... an alternative form of work done with youth that centres on the premise of intergenerational collaboration that might be described as located on the edge.*

This collaboration theory is reminiscent of Hart (1997) whose 'ladder of participation' model promotes an ideal of young people and adults sharing decisions (see *The type of place we were looking for: Radical youth work in practice* below). This idea is exemplified by Youth Force, a community action group in the Bronx, New York City (Checkoway et al., 2003). But the trouble with collaboration as an end in itself is that it assumes progressive political values on the part of the children and adults involved. Would collaboration between adult British National Party (BNP) activists and young people, leading to direct action and challenges to the status quo, count as radical youth work in this model?

Skott-Myhre and Gretzinger clearly argue from a left wing perspective, but their definition of radical youth work is based on methods rather than values.

The tendency for educators on the left to fudge their values led Freire (1998: 93) to argue:

> *I cannot be a teacher and be in favour of everyone and everything. I cannot be in favour merely of people, humanity, vague phrases far from the concrete nature of human practice.*

Youth workers are often guilty of this vagueness. This might partly be because of a strong belief in 'being non-judgmental'. At best, this prevents stereotyping and negative labelling, but at worst can stifle debate. Struggles against sexism and racism, however, have successfully changed youth work discourse and practice. I do not claim that youth work is always anti-sexist and anti-racist, but the overt sexist or racist comments and actions which were once common in youth clubs are becoming rarer. While these forms of youth work have at times been contradictory or ineffective, they are at least refreshingly clear about their political values. They demonstrate that we do make judgements. Indeed, not to make professional judgements makes us firstly apolitical, secondly more or less redundant, as in effect we would have given up the responsibilities consistent with the youth worker role and have become little more than a sounding board and/or a relatively unresponsive onlooker. Thirdly, if we fail to make professional judgements this quite logically means we are potentially unprofessional as it would compromise our child protection, health and safety functions as well as prevent us from taking action on bullying and all the various forms of bigotry that our job descriptions and obligations to policy and legislation dictate that we challenge, actively engage with, counter and prevent.

My working definition, then, is based on values (which I admit could be accused of being 'vague phrases'; it's difficult to avoid this in a short definition). It aims to include various left wing or anarchist political positions but not be so broad as to encompass 'everything except the right'. My definition also includes fun and points out the inevitability and necessity of political struggle. It is inevitably imperfect, but is at least a basis for this chapter and for wider debate:

A definition of radical youth work practice

Radical youth workers work informally with young people and take them seriously. Their daily work is informed by political and moral values: opposition to capitalism and authoritarianism, belief in equality and respect for the environment. They question 'common sense' and reflect critically on their work. They are aware that practising their beliefs will involve debate and struggle, but try to have fun too!

Controllers or liberators? Radical influences on youth work struggles

This section focuses on struggles in youth work history, and whether radicals have had influence on them. For the sake of brevity I will consider the radical influence on three key debates:

1. Is the purpose of youth work informal education or social control?
2. Does youth work worsen or tackle oppression and structural inequality?
3. How should youth work respond to 'new managerialism'?

Education or control?

The concept of informal education has become entwined with modern youth work discourse, but youth work's roots are in leisure provision, care and welfare. Nineteenth-century youth organisations such as the Boys Brigade, the Girls Friendly Society, Scouts and Guides used leisure activities to inculcate middle-class values (Davies, 1986) within a broadly compassionate environment wherein the well-being of young people was noted and sometimes attended to. Youth work jargon gives clues to these origins; the phrase 'youth provision' implies something provided by someone (middle-class adults) for someone else (working class young people).

Early youth work was a response to fears of working class 'disorder', and aimed to prepare young people for war and the workplace. After the introduction of the state-sponsored Youth Service in 1939 and its strengthening in 1960, youth workers have increasingly, particularly over the last quarter of a century, named at least part of their role as involving informal education (Davies, 1986). Over the last decade some practitioners have defined themselves almost wholly as playing this role and practically abandoned the title of youth worker. This conceptual change from the involvement in leisure time to educational delivery was pragmatic as well as ideological but it also appealed to professional ego, providing what some workers saw as a higher status role; educators attract higher pay and status than leisure workers and police officers (Leigh and Smart, 1985). At the same time in the early 1980s it was beneficial for youth work trainers and academics to identify themselves (their departments or colleges) as educational (rather than say welfare oriented) in order to take advantage of the then higher rates of pay in Higher

Education (relative to Further Education at that time). Hence the academic writers on youth work were quick to take up the educational signpost. Thus most writing about the informal educator role is perhaps best read circumspectly.

In a review of training, Butters and Newell (1978) argued that most youth work was part of the 'Social Education Repertoire' and as such had made a 'critical break' with character-building aims. They even called for the further radicalisation of youth work (a call which is less common in recent state-funded research reports!). In any case, Butters and Newell gave the impression that socially controlling forms of youth work had all but ended. Several years later, Taylor (1987: 133) argued that this had been over stated:

> . . . contrary to what liberal ideologies might wish to be true, character building, the indoctrination of obedience to the capitalist imperative, is alive and flourishing.

Capitalism was well entrenched in the youth work of the 1970s and 1980s, not only through 'character building' but also through its involvement in work-related skill courses and job creation schemes (Davies, 1979).

Many youth club members today remain blissfully unaware that they are meant to be getting an education, assuming that workers merely 'wield the keys and distribute the table tennis balls' (Davies, 1977: 4) – this of course begs the question if what is delivered is in fact 'education' or more a form of covert indoctrination – can one be said to 'authentically' taking part in 'education' without knowing it?.

Meanwhile, the state has attempted to formalise youth work's educational role by introducing a curriculum, unpopular with young people and youth workers (e.g. Stanton, 2004). This 'official blessing' of youth work, as being primarily or even wholly educational, is problematic for those seeking to formulate, or deliver, radical youth work, if they take on the now state-sanctioned educational role. Can a truly radical form of youth work implicate itself with a purpose approved and energised by the state? Radical youth work surely requires practitioners to define their own role and purpose that would surely be much more eclectic than a purely educational function. How can the youth worker/educator, as defined by state policy and the broadly liberal/reformist literature, be anything other than reactionary?

Alliance and compliance with the state pulls the profession towards a controlling role that is supplementary to control of the school. For example, recent government policy (DfES, 2002) requires youth workers to measure their members' achievements through recorded and accredited outcomes. Tiffany's (2007) research found that even detached youth work[1] is becoming structured, thereby excluding the most vulnerable young people it sets out to reach. As Jeffs (1997: 164) argues:

---

[1] Detached youth work is youth work which takes place flexibly on streets, in cafes, in shopping centres or wherever young people are (Tiffany 2007).

The provision of quantifiable output measures for youth work is impossible; for who can measure the worth of a conversation, the value of an experience or the depth of an insight, on a scale of one to ten?

Specifically radical influences on these debates are hard to detect, possibly because the fairly united (if muted) opposition by youth workers to social control policy has blurred boundaries between liberals and the left.

Equalising or oppressive?

Radical influences are more easily seen in anti-oppressive youth work. This includes youth work that is aimed at challenging homophobia, classism and disablism (albeit limited in some cases), but I will focus on anti-racist and feminist youth work. Williams (1988: 1) explores these tensions from a black neo-Marxist perspective, arguing that the state and white youth workers perceive black workers as a means of controlling black young people. This is of course in line with colonial forms of control that deployed 'trustee natives' to control their compatriots; how else could a few thousand British colonial troops and officials control the teaming millions of the Indian sub-continent in the 19th and early 20th century? Williams argues that success in these terms means:

> . . . we alienate ourselves from our communities, because we have to repress to a greater extent. It is one of the principle ways that we can show we are not a threat to the white system.

This is not confined to black workers/and young people. Youth work has made a habit of employing 'locals' of every creed and hue to work with their communities.

John's (1981) Youth and Race research project concluded that youth work was institutionally racist, working from a pathological view of black young people, and trying to control or exclude them. Radical black activists have been at the forefront of developing youth work practice that explicitly aims to change the system rather than support the status quo (John, 1981; Williams, 1998). Inevitably, the state has attempted to limit this effect, using 'divide and rule tactics' (that can be identified as a feature of the European colonial period – see Fanon, 1965 and 1967) to make groups compete for funding rather than work together.

Early 20th-century 'girls work' varied from the conservative, emphasising motherhood and marriage, to the feminist, promoting knowledge of social issues and lobbying for more rights for working women (Turnbull, 2001). By the early 1960s, most 'girls clubs' had become mixed and dominated by boys, while single gender boys clubs continued to operate. This led to feminist critiques which accused youth work of inherent sexism (NOW, 1983). In the 1980s, women feminists started groups specifically for young women, facilitated discussions on sexism and challenged unequal access to resources (e.g. Pons, 1981) while some male workers explored feminist approaches to boys work (e.g. Taylor, 1981). Openly feminist youth work has declined, partly because of negative perceptions of feminism (Spence, 2003) and partly because resources continue to favour supposedly criminal young men. The limited resources for young women are often for teenage pregnancy reduction, as young women tend to be perceived as sexually rather than criminally deviant. However, many of the formally 'boys only' clubs have, since the late 1970s become mixed gender facilities partly thanks to the feminist male youth workers who pioneered this change, but also the decreasing will of a growingly 'co-educational' era to resource this type of work together with the demise of its funding streams from the ostensibly shrinking bastions of sexism alongside their diminishing overt influence of society. However, these kind of cankers are far from extinct and have become largely camouflaged within institutional structures (this is evident from statistics on relative pay, the comparative paucity of women in authority positions, even in the upper echelons of the youth work whose workforce is predominately female etc.).

Responses to new managerialism

'New managerialism' has been a growing influence on public services during the Thatcher, Major and Blair years. Youth work has been affected later than most, somewhat protected by its traditional role as the 'Cinderella service' where under funding is accompanied by relative autonomy from state and market (Jeffs, 1997) – although in practice this separation has become much less convincing over the last dozen or so years. But managerialism increasingly affects youth work, introduced through apparently generous funding with strings attached. 'Diversion- ary activities' (under various policy guises) have enabled youth projects to organise attractive and expensive activities which were previously unaffordable. In return they are asked to target certain named individuals (or 'target groups') and keep detailed personal records on them which are often shared with other agencies. Opposition to this monitoring and surveillance has been limited; as generic youth work faces cuts, many youth workers have had to choose between colluding with the new managerialism or facing the closure of their projects.

Meanwhile, marketisation of youth work is heralded in the familiar guise of choice:

> *Our first challenge is to put young people themselves in control of the things to do and places to go in their area. We don't want government agencies second guessing them. So we propose to put buying power directly in the hands of young people themselves . . .*

DfES, 2005: 5

This means 'Youth Opportunity Cards' to be topped up by parents and local government to access facilities, including youth projects. These cards may increase choice for middle class young people who can afford expensive activities, but offer nothing to the most vulnerable: 'This subsidy would be withheld from young people engaging in unacceptable and anti-social behaviours and the card suspended or withdrawn' (op cit.: 5). This signals a change 'from a membership to a consumerist model of youth work' (Jeffs and Smith, 2006: 25) that in fairness has always been around in one guise or another but never as so ubiquitously as today. Again, there are few signs of active resistance except perhaps from trade unionists:

> The Youth Service could be bought and sold by young people swinging their new Opportunity Card in the direction of terrified councillors. If the young people misbehave of course their rights to cheap McDonalds and political influence in the Council House will be taken away. Whatever!
>
> Nicholls, 2005: 9

Summary

I have looked briefly at some important struggles in youth work history but missed out many others, including young people's struggles against youth work (Humphries, 1981; John, 1981; Ball and Ball 1973). While there has not been a coherent radical tendency, there is evidence of scattered radical involvement in struggles over the direction and role of youth work, particularly in anti-oppressive youth work. One common thread is that youth work has been most successfully controlled through resource allocation. It is unclear whether radical youth work has diminished, but there is a worrying lack of concerted opposition to current repressive youth work policy and the growing move towards replacing the same with forms of informal education, a practice unlike 'generic youth work' whose methodology and agenda makes room for focused state aims and so measurement of the same/standardised quality assurance.

Many youth workers are willingly joining the managerial recuperation of youth work, and those that do not are treated with suspicion (Jeffs and Smith, 2006). Apple's (2001: 30) reflections on similar struggles in schooling strike a chord:

> Active professionals are free to follow their entrepreneurial urges – as long as they 'do the right thing' . . . Foucault's panoptican is everywhere.

'The type of place we were looking for': Radical youth work in practice

Practical examples of radical youth work are limited in number but they are qualitatively important. To give an analogy, anti-climate change action happens at various levels including through governments, the media and pressure groups. Radical direct action groups are qualitatively different from other campaigners in both their methods and values, despite often receiving less media attention. By blocking the Drax power station and calling for it to be permanently closed, protesters acted themselves instead of asking for government action, drawing attention to the major changes they argue are needed to halt climate change (Indymedia, 2006). Similarly, radical practice has been a minority aspect of youth work but its methods and values are distinct. I will consider three areas where radicals have had an impact: political education, autonomous spaces and environmental youth work.

Political education

Magnuson (2005: 164) argues that political education is more often reformist than radical:

> *Instead of politics, we have created niches where we allow youth to participate, and we have created new languages, for example, civic engagement, character education, and public work. These niches and languages distract us – and youth – from participation in decisions about substantive political issues, and they allow us to avoid the real conflicts and divides that are part of politics.*

However, radical youth workers have sometimes created "opportunities for lived democracy: those tiny, small pockets where real democracy grows" (Jeffs, 2002: 8). Genuine participation in youth projects can give young people confidence to engage in wider political issues; one group for example became "a force to be reckoned with. They don't sit back and take what is handed out to them" (worker in Flowers, 1998: 40). Hart (1997) argues that young people can participate at different levels and that it is better to involve them in real decisions rather than simulating involvement in structures which are unlikely to listen to them. Examples of youth workers supporting meaningful youth involvement in local politics include Youth Force in the Bronx (Checkoway et al., 2003) and the Lewisham Young Mayor project (Binvolved, 2007). Incidentally, it is arguable that youth parliaments have been part of this. However, there is a growing number of young people and youth workers identifying them as little more than acts of tokenism and this has been a political lesson in itself (see Middleton, 2006). Tom Utley (2007) described them as 'sublimely fatuous'. Richard Pushman (2007) claimed that young people from marginalised groups are under-represented. A report by the Office of Public management, commissioned by the Department for Education and Skills (2004) was critical of UKYP's relationship with Scotland, Northern Ireland and Wales. See also http://unicef.org.uk/youthvoice/rights . . . interview.asp. particularly *How do you use the CRC in your daily life?*

Anti-oppressive youth work practice tends to be claimed as radical, but this is not necessarily so (Jeffs and Smith, 2003). Spence (2003) found that many young women's workers refused the label feminist and adopted political moderation as a survival strategy. John (1981) and Williams (1988) found that young people in many black-led youth projects were more politically aware than their youth workers. However, small voluntary organisations in particular have taken radical approaches to anti-oppressive issues. The Hideaway in Moss Side, Manchester was set up in the 1970s to counter negative perceptions of Moss Side and its black young people. As well as providing social activities, the centre was active in struggles against police violence and racism and was seen as a safe space for black young people during the riots. The Water Adventure Centre, also in Manchester, uses canoeing and water-based play as a basis for youth work and is locally known for its successful feminist work (WAC undated, Pons, 1981).

Autonomous spaces

Libertarian schools such as Summerhill (Neill, 1960) inspired various projects where young people had a high level of autonomy. Marie Paneth was an early pioneer of such spaces, running a children's project during the London blitz with few rules and minimal adult direction. She explained, 'I never interfered with their work, except that I met every attempt to produce anything at all, with approval' (Paneth, 1944: 10). Paneth was an early advocate of adventure playgrounds, which were at their most popular in the 1960s and 1970s. These were areas of often derelict land supervised by adults whose role was to acquire building materials, look after tools and dissuade bullying (Lambert and Pearson, 1974). Although adventure playgrounds were aimed at younger children, teenagers sat on the edges smoking and talking. The freedom of the playgrounds was at odds with their everyday lives, as this teenager found,

> *I found that far from settling down to study, as I should, I was restless through lack of freedom I suppose and felt rebellious towards school rules.*
>
> Jakki Hall in Lambert and Pearson, 1974: 75

The Paint House was an independent youth club run by two youth workers from an anarchist perspective. The workers encouraged local young people to use the space, hoping they would take responsibility for it. A group of 'skinheads' adopted the building, repeatedly trashing and re-building it, eventually realising it was an opportunity to have a space of their own.

> *When we first come 'ere you told us that this was our place, to do what we liked but we didn't believe you. We tried to force you to tell us what to do . . . we didn't realise that this was the type of place we were looking for.*
>
> young person in Daniel and McGuire, 1972: 55

The workers used the anti-authoritarian values they shared with the young people as a focus but were less effective where values clashed such as on racism. The group members eventually became less racist through relationships with the workers, but in the meantime the building was a safe space for active racists. The balance between autonomy and authority is an inevitable dilemma in this type of youth work. Even the much eulogised Summerhill was at times a haven for subtle forms of bullying (partly revealed in Channel 4's *Cutting Edge* documentary *Summerhill at 70*, first broadcast on 30 March 1992). Other self-run youth projects sprung up in the 1970s and 1980s, often inspired by the Punk movement. For a time it was not unheard of for young people to run youth clubs, hold keys or be allowed to sleep overnight (Daniel and McGuire, 1972; Leigh and Smart, 1985, personal conversations). Such freedoms are difficult to imagine in the contemporary era of the institutional control mechanisms implicit in risk assessment, inspection, litigation and financial regulation.

Environmental youth work

Although the environment has been a significant focus of radical political activity in the last 20 years, this has not been reflected in youth work. Despite calls for an increase in environmental youth work (Banks, 1993; Dearling and Armstrong, 1997) this has so far not transpired. Edbrooke (1993) encountered a widespread assumption that environmental education should be confined to schools, although schools tend to concentrate on factual information which fails to change children's behaviour (Morris and Shagen, 1996). Francique (2007) suggests that youth workers feel under-informed about the environment. Connelly (1993) argued that 'issues' such as recycling do not greatly interest most young people, whereas engaging young people in taking action on their surroundings attracts more attention.

Where the environment does appear in youth work, it is usually perceived as uncontroversial rather than as potentially radical (Banks, 1993). Francique (2007: 15) shows a reformist perspective to environmental youth work when she writes, 'What is required is merely a shift in approach rather than a major reorientation'. Others are more controversial. Dearling and Armstrong (1997: 3) ask:

> Should youth work stick to the 'safe' areas such as recycling and tree planting, or can empowerment embrace the Do it Yourself culture of the road and tree protesters?

Hart (1997) argues that children are likely to be more willing than adults to act on environmental issues because they are less vested in economic systems and spend more time in their local areas.

> There is considerable theoretical reason to believe that concern for the environment is based on an affection that can only come from autonomous, unmediated contact with it.
>
> Hart, 1997: 20

Groups such as the Woodcraft Folk and Wild Things in Nottinghamshire approach environmental youth work from a social equality perspective (the former since its foundation in 1925) aiming to encourage wider access to varied environments and outdoor activities (Wild Things, 2007; Davis, 2000).

Summary

While these examples of radical youth work practice may seem marginal, it is worth remembering that youth workers themselves have 'scant resources with which to challenge the status quo, and can only try to do their best to equip young people to cope with or resist it' (Beresford and Beresford, 1980: 19). These examples bring into sharp focus the dilemmas that are an inevitable aspect of radicalism. Can we engage in state-sponsored initiatives like the participation agenda from a critical rather than a conformist perspective? Are libertarian projects still possible, and can we give experiences of freedom without condoning oppressive beliefs and actions? Why have environmental issues not been a significant focus for struggle and resistance? Radical youth work seems to ask more questions than it answers.

'A tightrope we walk daily . . .' Experiences of youth work

For radical youth workers, everyday practice is 'a tightrope we walk daily, quite often losing our balance, and we only manage to maintain our grip by our fingertips' (Williams, 1988: 117). So far I have neglected this day to day reality; in this section I will redress the balance by reflecting on some of my own experiences. As Richardson (1990: 13) argues, 'much of our experience in education is ODTAA – one damn thing after another'. One way of communicating this complexity of everyday events is through fictional or narrative forms (Clough, 2002; Richardson, 1990). My narrative passages are not fictional, but I find that using aspects of this form enables me to focus on certain details and skip over others without simplifying the issues involved. As Davies argues, practice is often 'the result of improvisation, of expediency, of compromise, even of opportunism' (Davies, 1986: 13). Therefore, rather than selecting 'successful' or representative examples of my experience I have simply chosen memories which illustrate some dilemmas in radical youth work.

> Fifteen teenagers huddle by a local landmark, uncertain and expectant behind their cardboard signs ('SAVE OUR YOUTH SERVICE'). 'Did you just happen to be in town shopping too, then?' asked a colleague, smiling. I smiled back but to tell the truth I was surprised at the question. It has come to something when we can't even admit to supporting young people who want to protect their youth centres and our jobs. Are advocacy and community action no longer part of youth work? I used to joke that a measure of good youth work was whether the young people were fighting the council over something or another. The joke's not funny now. My manager was scared to put up a poster about this protest. Instead, our youth centre walls are decorated with motivational posters demanding pride in our employer even as it makes our colleagues redundant.

I do not wish to blame my colleagues for being cautious; they were brave to support the young organisers of this protest and I believe some were reprimanded. But it's hard to fight for something without admitting you are doing so; it is hard to be an effective activist while hiding. In this case I asserted my right to attend this protest in my own time and refused to lie about why I was there, but I am a very junior employee and can get away with it easier than my managers. At other times I have been more cautious. I've never told this next story to other youth workers, and I am interested in what readers might think . . .

> *I was due in court for ripping up genetically modified crops. The young people were indignant that I'd taken a day off in the middle of the summer programme, so I told them and my co-worker about the court case and they all decided to come to court to support me. I was surprised, delighted, but a bit worried how it would look to my manager – and (accidentally on purpose) I never got around to telling him. The astonished look on the usher's face was priceless as twelve black young people entered the public gallery of that small-town-white courtroom. The youngest were escorted out; none of us knew that 'minors' are not allowed in court. The hearing lasted all of ten minutes, but back home we talked for days: should children be allowed to watch court cases; why did I break the law; should people with criminal records become youth workers; what it's like being arrested? I still think this was good youth work . . . but the episode didn't get a mention in my summer report!*

I am unconvinced by my excuses for dishonesty (hiding); I had trustworthy colleagues I could have discussed my decision with. Other types of youth worker dishonesty include 'talking the talk' while doing very little. I have met some politically aware people who talk for hours about problems with government youth policy, institutional sexism or racism in the youth service, and how the bosses know nothing. And yet, there are only a few youth workers I have had these conversations with and then gone out and done a satisfying night of youth work.

> *'Forgot my coat' she said, and I wondered if her half-smile was in apology or smug satisfaction at getting one over on me. Eight times I had cycled cold miles to this echoing community centre to work at a mythical youth club, and I hadn't met one young person. My new colleagues worried me, so satisfied as they were moaning about how they and the local young people had been done wrong by the council in the past. Now they collected their wages as some kind of compensation for how they'd been messed about, and they certainly weren't impressed at having me imposed on them, a naïve southerner suggesting that we walk around the estate and get to know some young people for once.*

I've experienced and heard versions of this story many times. But what should be done? The 'new managerial' response would include support and supervision, clear targets and disciplinary action 'as a last resort'. As an anarchist I automatically side with workers against management, but I believe in youth work and get frustrated at colleagues' laziness. Some argue that the council does not own them, so why should they work harder than necessary? My energetic enthusiasm makes me a productive employee; am I the radical? My involvement in youth work is part of my political action in the world whereas for others, it is a job to be skived like any other.

Unless I achieve political change through my youth work, who decides who's right and wrong?

> *'Teamwork'; a word popular in workplaces and youth clubs. I'm suspicious of its managerial overtones, and yet remember wistfully a time when I really felt like part of a team. Each week, several detached youth workers got together to share experiences and discuss things that affected us, from local policies and funding to wider political issues affecting young people and ourselves as workers. Our manager encouraged critical reflection and sprinkled our discussions with theories from Freire and Foucault. These sessions were powerful; I was on the edge of my seat! Our manager encouraged us to take up training opportunities and go to university; to see ourselves as educators and to educate ourselves too. He trusted us, and showed it by dividing the project's budget between us. I have never before or since heard of part-time youth workers being given such financial autonomy. But it was collective autonomy: we answered not just to our manager and the young people we worked with, but also in each weekly meeting we answered to our peers.*

This 'collective autonomy' approach could address laziness and incompetence, but this would serve reactionary as well as radical aims. While some methods may be suited to radical practice, it is values which distinguish it. This is of course the case with all youth work. An example from my experience is the Streetmates group who got together to have a say in the regeneration of their local area. The power and success of this group was that the motivation came from the young people themselves and that their objectives were supported by us youth workers. (If the same young people had wanted to set up a community group to stop asylum seekers from living in their area, I'd have taken a dissuasive role rather than an encouraging one.)

Inevitably I have only skimmed the surface of some of the dilemmas I have struggled with in my own practice. I use my personal experience with the awareness that, 'Historically, it is too often those who seek to liberate who are the most self-deceptive about their own motives' (Magnuson, 2005: 165). Honest critical reflection shared with our peers should go some way to preventing this. As well as oral discussions and academic writing, I am interested in the use of narrative to celebrate and criticise youth work practice from a radical perspective. As Richardson (1990: 101) argues:

> *Racism and nationalism are kept alive through narratives as well as through structures, and we need – amongst other things – our own oppositional narratives in order to deal with them.*

Conclusion – taking sides

This would have been easier to write had my focus been on criticising the myriad capitalist influences on youth work rather than looking for the few radical ones. I wanted to find possibilities and hope, but found my optimism tested. Despite wearing rose-tinted spectacles I did not find it easy to reclaim radical theory and practice, possibly because its history is scattered and barely recorded, its theories vague and its practice contradictory. However, as long as I remain a youth worker I intend to test the potential of radical theory and practice. The alternative is to stand by as youth workers become indistinguishable from other soft-cop public employees such as community wardens, police support officers and neighbour nuisance mediators (versions of which seem to be the state ambitions for community and informal education as professional ends in themselves). These professions have little space for the radical values I identified above (*Towards a theory of 'radical' youth work*, see Chapter 7), 'opposition to capitalism and authoritarianism, belief in equality and respect for the environment'. I believe there is still room for the practice of these values in youth work.

This conclusion builds on discussions in previous sections to propose some key dilemmas and possibilities for future attempts at radical youth work practice. The dilemmas are questions which the writing of this chapter has brought into sharp focus for me. Although I have strong feelings about the issues they raise, they are dilemmas because I cannot yet see a clear way forward. The possibilities are my proposals for radical youth workers, guidelines I intend to test out in my future practice. Although I will use the inclusive pronoun 'we' to refer to those who identify with the definition of radical youth work I proposed in *Towards a theory of 'radical' youth work*, I do not mean to assume common agreement. I suggest rather that these dilemmas and possibilities would benefit from further discussion and debate.

Five dilemmas

1. Can we be principled and work for the state?
Youth workers hide behind the excuse that we support young people in what they want rather than acting on our own values (Flowers, 1998). This is nonsensical unless we only work with young people we broadly agree with; I have yet to meet a youth worker who helped young fascist sympathisers with their leaflet distribution. If radicalism includes taking sides against structural forces of capitalism and state control, shouldn't we openly make our judgements and act as strongly against these as we (should) do against racism? The dilemma is that youth work has been subsumed into capitalism. Fighting this would mean opposing systems that our jobs require us to comply with such as the direct surveillance of young people through computerised monitoring systems.

2. Can we challenge common sense?
New managerialism in youth work is culturally enforced through the tyranny of 'good practice'. Things which were debateable are now the norm: minor health and safety risks override freedom to develop innovative projects and young people's

need for exciting, demanding experiences; monitoring requirements undermine confidentiality, and accredited 'benchmarks' challenge the principle of informality. Just as we encourage young people to think critically, we too need to think for ourselves, questioning and debating the new common sense. As with the previous dilemma, taking action on these issues could be more daunting.

3. How do we balance principles and funding?

The state controls youth workers most effectively through the targeting of resources rather than through compulsory reforms (see Chapter 7 *Controllers or liberators? Radical influences on youth work struggles* above). There is no clear solution for youth workers fearing for their jobs or attracted by improved facilities, but this question cannot be dodged. Many of us are seduced by offers of funding, becoming materialist in the guise of 'getting what's best for the young people'. To maximise our freedom from the state, we may need to explore how to run independent youth projects without funding, but would this mean doing the state's job for free?

4. How can radical youth workers avoid disillusionment?

Burn out and exhaustion affect youth workers of all political perspectives. Radicals experience particular stress because we constantly negotiate the contradictions between our deeply felt convictions and the policies and practices of our employers. If we voice our opinions and act on our principles we are labelled as 'troublemakers' and risk our funding, job or status. In addition, it is inevitably stressful to live in a world which is far from how we would like it to be. And yet, without hope we become disillusioned and ineffective.

5. Can youth work ever change anything?

Youth work in itself has changed little on a structural level. At best, our actions are small-scale and their consequences might only become apparent years later. One possibility is to remain involved in other political activism as well as being a youth worker. The success of youth work as political action relies heavily on feminist 'personal is political' theories. Structural change, on the other hand, may be supported by radical youth work but is unlikely to result from it. This can make daily practice feel rather hollow.

Five possibilities

1. Developing collective autonomy as workers

Collective autonomy means exploiting freedoms and spaces as we find them, but as part of a community rather than as unaccountable mavericks. We should create collectives at different levels, from our own work teams to national networks. Different types of existing networks include trade unions, the Federation for

Detached Youth Work and the Critical Chatting group.[2] As part of networks we can discuss and debate ideas and take joint action. Being part of a collective can address burn out and isolation, and reduces the ease with which individual 'troublemakers' can be targeted by the state.

2. Developing collective autonomy among young people

Autonomous spaces are among the most important things youth work can offer. This does not mean we should let young people do everything they want, but we could explicitly aim to make youth clubs available for young people to use with some degree of freedom and self organisation. Play workers talk of providing 'compensatory space' for children who have few opportunities for freedom and adventure in today's society. Teenagers (and adults) need play and adventure too, but society curtails this impulse even more strongly than in younger children. We should create spaces which compensate for the authoritarianism young people meet everywhere they go, not seem to be more of the same.

3. Educating ourselves

In recent years, youth work theorists have increasingly argued the need to learn from history (Gilchrist et al., 2001, 2003; Davies, 1986). There has been a growth in written history and discussion forums such as the History of Community and Youth Work conferences.[3] We should engage in these conferences, read relevant literature, and youth workers should reflect and write about their own experiences and histories. Those of us who are interested in theory should explore alternative ways to share this interest, not confine it to documents that most youth workers don't have the time or the inclination to read.

4. Educating young people

Most radicals agree that youth work aims to educate, but for what? Our 'curriculum' (can a curriculum be informal? – the word informal comes from New Latin meaning 'course') should be powerful, not pointless. This could include learning how authority structures work sharing skills of political involvement, exploring the environment and history of local areas, and learning about inequalities and environmental destruction. If we fail to move beyond the constraints of schooling (*Deschooling Society*, Ilich, 1971) what is the point of using the tool of informal education? We need to consider our reasons for doing any work that is neither excitingly educational nor the practice of autonomy and adventure.

5. Regaining our commitment to youth work

While the concept of wage labour is problematic to me as an anarchist, I would choose to spend time in dialectical activity with teenagers even in my utopian

---

[2] See for example www.cywu.org.uk, www.unison.org.uk/localgov/youthcommunity.asp, www.detachedyouth-work.info, http://critically-chatting.0catch.com
[3] See http://www.infed.org/events/history_conference_2007.htm

post-revolutionary society. Even for those who would not, it is worth finding something to commit to in youth work for the sake of ourselves and the young people we work with. Workers who would rather be in their garden could fill their youth club with plants and grow vegetables in window boxes. Those who dream of the forest or the sea might take young people there whenever they can. As well as following young people's existing interests youth work could also work with them to broaden their horizons, and using our own interests is consistent with this. It might also be a way for some of us to commit to youth work once more.

The theory and practice of radical youth work is scattered, messy and contradictory, but this does not excuse sitting on the fence. History shows that a passive response to government interventions has resulted in youth work becoming increasingly embroiled in the capitalist project, latterly by the seeming state intention to remould it exclusively into bourgeois and reactionary interpretations of informal and community education routes. In pursuit of funding, or simply to follow the latest guidelines, we increasingly monitor and control the most vulnerable young people, or lose contact with those young people, by concentrating on accreditation and formal programmes. History also shows that radical workers can influence the direction of youth work as well as organising projects for freedom and against authoritarianism, for the environment and against capitalism, for equality and against oppression. Through dialectic with colleagues and young people, we need to work out which side we are on. Unless we want capitalism and social control to become permanently entrenched in youth work by way of state sanctioned and monitored 'education' that are in reality propaganda and the means of indoctrination, neutrality is not an option!

Acknowledgements

Hundreds of conversations with young people, friends, family and colleagues have informed my thinking before and during the writing of these pages. Significant conversations often remain unacknowledged unless given the title 'interview'. Any list would be too short to include all those I've spoken with about youth work and radical politics.

However, I particularly want to mention colleagues at Bath Development Education Centre, the A6 Detached Project (Manchester) and the Water Adventure Centre (Manchester), projects in which critical debate was encouraged. Similarly, staff and participants at Manchester University's Community Work Unit have been vital influences on my thinking and work.

References

Altrichter, H. (1993) The Concept of Quality in Action Research: Giving Practitioners a Voice in Educational Research. In Schratz, M. (Ed.) *Qualitative Voices in Educational Research*. Falmer.

Apple, M. (2001) *Educating The 'Right' Way: Markets, Standards, God and Inequality*. Routledge Falmer.

Ball, C. and Ball, M. (1973) *Education For a Change: Community Action and The School.* Penguin.

Banks, S. (1993) Young People and The Environment: An Editorial. *Youth And Policy*, 42: 1–5.

Beresford, S. and Beresford, P. (1980) Powerless in Toytown. *Youth In Society*, 49: 18–9.

Bettelheim, B. (1979) The Ignored Lesson of Anne Frank, in *Surviving and Other Essays.* Knopf.

Binvolved (2007) http://www.Binvolved.org.uk/ Accessed 1/5/07

Bond, A. (Ed.) (2004) *Writing Your Masters Thesis.* Bishops Lydeard: Studymates.

Bradford, S. (1997) The Management of Growing up: Young People in Community Settings. In Roche, J. and Tucker, S. (Eds.) *Youth in Society.* Sage.

Butters, S. and Newell, S. (1978) *Realities of Training: A Review of The Training of Adults Who Volunteer to Work With Young People in The Youth and Community Service.* National Youth Board.

Checkoway, B., Figueroa, L. and Richards-Schuster, K. (2003) Democracy Multiplied in an Urban Neighbourhood: Youth Force in The South Bronx. *Children, Youth and Neighbourhoods*, 13: 2, Accessed 8/4/07 At http://Colorado.Edu/Journals/Cye

Clough, P. (2002) *Narratives and Fictions in Educational Research.* Open University Press.

Clough, P. and Nutbrown, C. (2002) *A Student's Guide to Methodology: Justifying Enquiry.* Sage.

Connelly, D. (1993) Environmental Youth Work: Making Connections. *Youth and Policy*, 42: 44–9.

Daniel, S. and McGuire, P. (Eds.) (1972) *The Paint House: Words From an East End Gang.* Penguin.

Davies, B. (1977) Agency Collaboration or Worker Control? Alternative Models For More Integrated Services to Young People. *Youth in Society*, 22: 3–6.

Davies, B. (1979) *From Social Education to Social and Life Skills Training: In Whose Interest?* Leicester: National Youth Bureau. (Accessed on 7/4/07 at http://www.Infed.Org/Archives/Bernard_Davies/Davies_In_Whose_Interests.htm)

Davies, B. (1986) *Threatening Youth: Towards a National Youth Policy.* Open University Press.

Davies, B. (2005) *Youth Work: A Manifesto For Our Times.* Leicester: National Youth Agency.

Davies, B. (2006) 'Threatening Youth' Revisited: Youth Policies Under New Labour. *The Encyclopaedia of Informal Education*, Accessed 25/1/07 at www.Infed.Org/Archives/Bernard_Davies/Revisiting_Threatening_Youth.htm

Davis, M. (2000) *Fashioning a New World: A History of The Woodcraft Folk.* Holyoake Books.

Dearling, A. and Armstrong, H. (1997) *Youth Action and The Environment.* Russell House Publishing.

DfES (2002) *Transforming Youth Work: Resourcing Excellent Youth Services.* Nottingham: DfES.

DfES (2005) *Youth Matters: Summary.* Nottingham: DfES.

Edbrooke, J. (1993) Policy Into Practice in Birmingham. *Youth and Policy*, 42: 38–43.

Fanon, F. (1965) *The Wretched of The Earth.* Macgibbon and Kee.

Fanon, F. (1967) *Black Skin, White Masks.* Grove Press.

Flowers, R. (1998) How Effective Are Youth Workers in Activating Young People's Voices? *Youth Studies Australia*, 17: 4, 34–40.

Francique, M. (2007) *Working With Young People to Create a Climate of Change*. National Youth Agency.

Freire, P. (1988) (Trans. Bergman Ramos, M.) *Pedagogy of The Oppressed.* Continuum.

Freire, P. (1998) *Pedagogy of Freedom: Ethics, Democracy and Civic Courage.* (Trans. Clarke, P.) Maryland: Rowman and Littlefield.

Freire, P. and Shor, I. (1987) *A Pedagogy For Liberation*. Macmillan.

Guardian (2006) BBC Unveils Radical Revamp of Website, Accessed 27/3/07 at *http:///Media.Guardian.co.uk/Site/Story/0,,1760999,00.html*

Gilchrist, R., Jeffs, T. and Spence, J. (Eds) (2001) *Essays in The History of Youth and Community Work.* Youth Work Press.

Gilchrist, R., Jeffs, T. and Spence, J. (Eds) (2003) *Architects of Change: Studies in The History of Community and Youth Work.* National Youth Agency.

Harris, P. (2005) *The Curriculum Debate and Detached Youth Work.* Accessed 12/02/07 at http://www.Detachedyouthwork.Info/Fdyw003.html

Hart, R. (1997) *Children's Participation: The Theory and Practice of Involving Young Citizens in Community Development and Environmental Care.* Earthscan.

Hicks, D. (2004) Radical Education. In Ward, S. (Ed.) *Education Studies: A Student's Guide.* Routledge Falmer.

Humphries, S. (1981) *Hooligans or Rebels? An Oral History of Working-Class Youth and Childhood 1889–1939.* Basil Blackwell.

Illich, I. (1971) *Deschooling Society.* Harper and Row.

Indymedia (2006) Climate Camp to Target UK's Largest Power Station. Accessed On 7th May 2007 At *http://Www.Indymedia.Org.Uk/En/2006/06/343155.Html*

Ivanic, R. and Simpson, J. (1992) Who's Who in Academic Writing? In Fairclough, N. (Ed.) *Critical Language Awareness.* Longman.

Jeffs, T. (1997) Changing Their Ways: Youth Work and The Underclass Theory. In Macdonald. R. (Ed.) *Youth, The 'Underclass' and Social Exclusion.* Routledge.

Jeffs, T. (2002) Whatever Happened to Radical Youth Work? *Concept*, 12: 2, 4–8.

Jeffs, T. and Smith, M. (1994) Young People, Youth Work and a New Authoritarianism. *Youth and Policy*, 46.

Jeffs, T. and Smith, M. (2003) Putting Youth Work in Its Place. In Nolan, P.C. (Ed.) *Twenty Years of Youth and Policy: A Retrospective.* National Youth Agency.

Jeffs, T. and Smith, M. (2006) Where is Youth Matters Taking Us? *Youth And Policy*, 91: 23–39.

John, G. (1981) In The Service of Black Youth. National Association of Youth Clubs.

Lambert, J. and Pearson, J. (1974) *Adventure Playgrounds.* Penguin.

Lambert, J. (1978) Political Values and Community Work Practice. In Curno, P. (Ed.) *Political Issues and Community Work.* Routledge and Kegan Paul.

Leigh, M. and Smart, A. (1985) *Interpretation and Change: The Emerging Crisis of Purpose in Social Education.* National Youth Bureau.

London-Edinburgh Weekend Return Group (1980) *In and Against The State.* Pluto.

Magnuson, D. (2005) Response to 'Captured by Capital'. *Child and Youth Care Forum*, 34: 2, 163–6.

Marx, K. (1845) *Thesis on Feuerbach.* Accessed 14/01/07 at http://www.Cpusa.Org/Article/Articleprint/487/

Meighan, R. and Siraj-Blatchford, I. (2003) *A Sociology of Educating.* Continuum.

Middleton, E. (2006) Youth Participation in The UK: Bureaucratic Disaster or Triumph of Child Rights? *Children, Youth and Environments*, 16: 2, 11.

Morris, M. and Shagen, I. (1996) *Green Attitudes or Learned Responses?* National Foundation For Educational Research.

National Organisation For Work With Girls and Young Women (1983)

Neill, A.S. (1960) *Summerhill.* Hart.

Nicholls, D. (2005) Youth Work Matters. *CYWU Rapport*, November: 8–10.

Office of Public Management (2004) Review of The UK Youth Parliament. Office of Public Management.

Paneth, M. (1944) *Branch Street.* The Women's Book Club. Allen and Unwin.

Pons, L. (1981) Water Adventure. *Youth in Society*, 59: 13–5.

Pushman, R. (2007) The Centre For Public Scrutiny Pdf/Review/5169.Pdf 'Involving Young People in Decision Making and Local Democracy' (PDF) Buckinghamshire County Council: Community and Environmental Services.

Reclaiming The Past. *Youth In Society*, 79: 18–9.

Richardson, R. (1990) *Daring to be a Teacher*. Trentham.

Richardson, R. (1996) *Fortunes and Fables: Education For Hope in Troubled Times*. Trentham.

Robertson, S. (2001) A Warm, Safe Place: An Argument For Youth Clubs, *Infed*, Accessed 6/2/07 At http://Www.Infed.Org/Archives/E-Texts/Robertson . . . Clubs.Htm

Shaw, M. (2003) 'Community', Community Work and The State. In Gilchrist, R., Jeffs, T. and Spence, J. (Eds.) (2003) *Architects of Change: Studies in The History of Community and Youth Work*. National Youth Agency.

Skott-Myhre, H. (2005) Captured by Capital: Youth Work and The Loss of Revolutionary Potential. *Child and Youth Care Forum*, 34: 2, 141–57.

Skott-Myhre, H. (2006) Radical Youth Work: Becoming Visible. *Child and Youth Care Forum*, 5:3, 9–229.

Skott-Myhre, H. and Gretzinger, M. (Undated) Creating a Politics of Mutual Liberation For Youth and Adults, Part 2.*Journal of Child and Youth Care Work*, 20: 110–27.

Smith, M. (2001) Josephine Macalister Brew: Youth Work and Informal Education. In Gilchrist, R., Jeffs, T. and Spence, J. (Eds.) *Essays in The History of Youth and Community Work*. Youth Work Press.

Spence, J. (2003) Feminism in Work With Girls and Young Women. In Nolan, P.C. (Ed.) *Twenty Years of Youth and Policy: A Retrospective*. National Youth Agency.

Spence, J., Pugh, C. and Turner, P. (2003) Reconfiguring Youth Work: Some Findings From The Joseph Rowntree Foundation Detached and Outreach Research Project. *Youth and Policy*, 81.

Stanton, N. (2004) The Youth Work Curriculum and The Abandonment of Informal Education. *Youth and Policy*, 85: 71–85.

Taylor, T. (1981) Challenging Stereotypes, Changing Roles . . . and Developing a Strategy, *Youth in Society*, 59: 18–20.

Taylor, T. (1987) Youth Workers as Character Builders: Constructing a Socialist Alternative. In Jeffs, T. and Smith. M. (Eds.) *Youth Work*. Macmillan.

Taylor, T. (2000) Beyond Connexions: A Response. *Infed*, Accessed On 03/02/07 At http://www.Infed.Org/Personaladvisers/Connexions-Ttaylor.htm

Taylor, T. (2007) *Youth Work and Class: The Struggle That Dare Not Speak Its Name*. Accessed At http://Critically-Chatting.0catch.Com/Recentarticles/Index.html

Thomas, D.N. (1978) Community Work, Social Change and Social Planning. In Curno, P. (Ed.) *Political Issues and Community Work*. Routledge and Kegan Paul.

Tiffany, G. (2007) *Standards and Excellence in Detached Youth Work*. The Federation For Detached Youth Work.

Turnbull, A. (2001) Gendering Young People: Work, Leisure and Girls Clubs: The Work of The National Organisation of Girls Clubs and Its Successors 1911–1961. In Gilchrist, R., Jeffs, T. and Spence, J. (Eds.) *Essays in The History of Youth and Community Work*. Youth Work Press.

Utley, T. (6 December 2007) Lack of Sex Education is Not The Problem. *Daily Mail*.

Water Adventure Centre (Undated) *Policy*. Manchester: WAC.

Wells, G. (1987) *The Meaning Makers*. Heinemann.

Wild Things (2007) About Wild Things. Accessed 07/05/07 At http://Www.Wildthings.Org.Uk/

Williams, L. (1988) *Partial Surrender: Race and Resistance in The Youth Service.* Lewes. Falmer Press.

Wright, N. (1989) *Assessing Radical Education.* Open University Press.

Wylie, T. (2001) 'Those That I Guard I do Not Love': A Memoir of HM Inspectorate and Youth Work in The Thatcher Era. In Gilchrist, R., Jeffs, T. and Spence, J. (Eds.) *Essays in The History of Youth and Community Work.* Youth Work Press.

Young, K. (1999) *The Art of Youth Work.* Russell House Publishing.

8

RAC: Regard, Accompaniment and Consideration

This chapter, while following the ethos and spirit of previous material, is included to demonstrate how critique might give rise to concrete and novel techniques that can be readily deployed in day to day practice. However, with the diminution and passing of the paradigm of informal and community education in youth work, practitioners will need to develop a new lexicon to house the rising, more relevant attitudes and values of emerging forms of progressive and radical practice.

What follows might be understood as part of this process, but also as an exemplar and encouragement for those in the field to begin to build and develop practice methodology in order to make their personal efforts in the professional context increasingly germane to their own unique work environment and client groups. It is hoped that this will work to undermine the 'one-size-fits-all' attitude to the delivery of practice technique; the reliance on dated models of group work (mostly informed by Cold War, West Coast American influences) and notions loosely premised on increasingly questionable quasi-psychoanalytic frameworks, built around a somewhat narcissistic subjectivism, generically labelled as 'reflection'.

Words and Concepts

In this chapter I want to provide some practice methodologies that confirm and enact the ethos and trajectory of the ideas and theory included in the discussions that make up this book. I'm going to look at a number of ideas and how they can be used in our work with young people. This will involve introducing a vocabulary that will help you make use of the theory that is going to be broached (by way of these ideas). I do not want to use words that seem to have one meaning but which are used to achieve something totally opposite to that overt meaning (see Chapter 6). So I'm going to make clear what it is I mean by the words I'm going to use. Many of the words you will come across in this first section explain a 'conceptual framework' for your practice. The words might be thought of as part of a technical language for our work that exists to put over ways of interacting with our clients. So, for example, we will be talking about 'consideration', which as a legal term means:

> . . . a promise to perform a certain act – for example, a promise to fix a leaky roof. Whatever its particulars, consideration must be something of value to the people who are making the contract.

This is not what I will be referring to when thinking about the 'concept' of consideration, but it is a useful word applied to a way of working with people.

As things stand, many of the concepts (the building blocks of theory) used in our practice and related areas are very dated and come from a quite under developed school of thought. Mostly, as ideas, their origins lie in the west coast America of the 1960s, a time that influenced many academics and writers who have had an impact on youth and community work and informal education. Words like 'relationship' are dropped in our work as if they explain the kind of connection we might have with those we work with. But as soon as you use a word like this it begs the question 'what kind of relationship?' Then we are involved in dealing with how a professional relationship differs and/or compares to say a friendship, or a sibling relationship. This invites us to ask things like 'is our relationship with our clients a bit like friendship'? And some practitioners claim to actually be friends with (having 'befriended') their clients – they even talk about 'celebrating' that they 'love all' their clients (you can discern the connection with the 'flower-power' generation here).

This invites enquiry about the quality of this friendship or 'love'. One person I recently talked to called it a 'low level friendship' although he didn't tell his client-friend that, which of course a low level friend wouldn't. But the person at the other end of this low level friendship will sooner or later recognise this status and any trust generated will be justifiably withdrawn.

Many of the people who talk about 'loving' their friend-clients also claim to be interested in 'feelings' and ask those they work with to talk about their feelings, as if this were a proven cure-all for life's problems (a notion that has been discredited somewhat in the last couple of decades or so – see Masson 1989). But the whole notion of 'talking about your feelings' seems to misunderstand 'feeling'; talk is talk and feelings are feelings – we feel our feelings! Talking about feelings is like talking about air. Talking about describing air isn't air. 'Analysing feelings' is a step further down the road of nonsense.

Words are the means by which we build concepts and we need to start to develop a means of expression that does not drag us along trails of sentiment and inappropriate attachment that set up improper expectations, dependencies or trails of sheer nonsensical meandering verbiage. We require words that can generate concepts that will fit with the work that we do and avoid detracting from that. We want to do a good, pragmatic job, that is focused and professional. We are not going to do this by adopting concepts that are complicit in us taking on the guise of a surrogate parent, therapist, councillor, lover, guru or friend and all the confusion and unfulfillable promises that are implicit in taking on facets of these identities.

I hope the pages that follow will go some way to removing such obstacles from your practice and provide you instead with some useful tools for your work.

Working with and learning from people

Something that is hardly ever noted when working with an individual is that it involves, at the same time, work with groups in some way. Even if you are working with just one person, you still have a group; you and the individual. Although there are those who will argue that a pair is not a group, this is navel gazing at its worst; splitting hairs for the sake of looking like a 'group work expert', the kind of person that anyone who values the precious minutes of their life would catch the last tug out of Babbleville to avoid. What we are interested in is the 'live' area that exists between people. If you ever visit a Japanese stone garden you will get some understanding of this idea. Often, when westerner's look at the stones of various sizes placed among a waterless pond of pebbles, they begin to look at the stones themselves in an attempt to decipher meaning or hit on a feeling that might be transmitted from the same. However, the energy of a stone garden lies not in the shape or positioning of the stones. The 'art' or 'merit' of the garden is generated out of the space between the stones; the shape, content and potential of that space.

It is this place, the apparent gap between objects and objects, people and objects, people and other people, where the 'ignition' for things that are going to happen comes from. That is what we are going to try to begin to understand – everything you will read is geared to acknowledging/perceiving this spark and exploring the consequences. This will offer us opportunities to find out about others but it should also provide us with lessons about ourselves.

The character of your work requires you to understand others and while this chapter will give you 'practice' in this, however, before one can understand others it is probably not a bad idea to develop your understanding of yourself.

You may feel you already know yourself. I'm sure you do. Most people have an idea of what they are like, some better than others. But we rarely get the chance to devote an appreciable amount of time to try this view of ourselves out on others. Again, one could say that we do this all the time in the course of our daily lives, and it would be hard to argue with this. However, those 'experiments' are secondary to other events and situations – we might be shopping or partying or having a row with a traffic warden.

What follows will give you the opportunity to do something quite unusual in that it is primarily about 'self study', even if at times it might ask you to think about the lives of others. That seems pretty straightforward, but where it gets a bit strange is that these 'other lives' will be asking you about your response to other people; chiefly those you work with and among. Hence there is more than you involved in this examination of self. It is not every day that we have time focused just on that task, developing our awareness of ourselves, others and how others might understand us. But for this to happen you will need to commit yourself to the process. You can cruise through the following pages on auto-pilot and get not very much from the journey. However, because you picked up this book and have read it thus far, I can assume that you are a relatively thoughtful person working on your own integrity and that needs to be regarded and honoured. The more you withdraw from the process this book has laid out for your use, the less you will get from the effort of reading it. In the same way, to use this chapter to develop your awareness and potential as a 'people worker' you will need to be fully part of the 'events' that follow.

The strange thing is that we are led to believe that individuals and groups are predictable, that after all is the basis of what has come to be known as 'group work' and some forms of psychotherapy. These 'activities' suggest that we can plan for what happens when we are with an individual or are part of a group. If you tap 'group work' into your search engine you will find this confirmed. But the proposal that a group of eight gay male pensioners in Islington next year will react to each other in a fairly similar way as a group of 15 young Pakistani women (between the ages of 14 and 19) did in Karachi in 1968 is, of course, patent nonsense. It is equally silly to say that a nomadic 46-year-old woman from Tibet, having lived in Penge for six weeks, is going to react in the same way to getting a letter from her solicitor as Gordon Brown might.

The accusation that people from a wide range of backgrounds are 'predictable', and that their behaviour can be categorised as if they were quite simple animals, is based on a 'deficit model'. People are taken to be less complicated or complex than they really are and this being the case, right from the start, gets us thinking, as the people who observe other people, who supposedly 'know' about them, and who record and interpret their behaviour, that we have something that they (those seen in deficit) don't have (professional expertise, knowledge, insight, understanding etc.). This does not really strike me as an altogether sound basis on which to promote ideals like equality and honesty and certainly it does not lay the ground for anything that might be called a 'trusting relationship'.

Ambitions to 'enable', 'facilitate' and' empower' also carry this 'deficit' problem (they start out from the premise that folk are 'less able' or lack power).

The way we are going to try to think about people (each other) is to do our best to see them not as 'things to interpret' but as:

- Human entities that are full of potential.
- Beings that can teach us about themselves as we teach them about ourselves.

When I go into a group or meet with an individual for the first time, they will be unlikely to be very keen to learn anything from me unless I am interested in learning from them. That is how I get to understand a person or a group (by them teaching me about them). As they teach me they get to know about me. It fascinates me how much quicker the process of mutual understanding works this way round – it is a much slower process, if it happens at all, when someone goes into a group with the idea that they will teach the group something, about themselves or anything else.

When a group is involved in this teaching, they not only begin to learn about you but as they teach you they learn about themselves as individuals and how they react in groups particularly this group. This might well be the start of a lifelong exploration because as soon as someone feels that someone else wants to know about them they usually begin to want to know about the person who is interested in them. This is the very foundation of trust.

Knowing uniqueness – unsafe places

When this process is in train, when it is working (and it doesn't work all the time – we are doing well if it even works some of the time that we are with people) then you get what I have come to think of as a 'virtuous circle'. The 'bog-standard' group or session with an individual begins to take on a totally unique personality of its own – the group will be like no other group and can't be compared to any other group (except in very shallow and insignificant ways). The conversation you have with the person will take on its own identity and might sometimes stay with you till you die.

It is accepting the person or the group as having this uniqueness that opens the potential for the person or the group to value itself as 'inimitable', because it starts to recognise its own life – each individual in the group becomes the midwife to the group as a phenomenon all of its own.

It is at this point that delicate flowers like 'trust' and 'care' can be grown. It is an environment wherein people can begin to express themselves not within some manufactured idea of 'safety', but build a place capable of sustaining and supporting 'risk' – expressing oneself is not a 'safe' activity, neither is the giving of trust – trust has to be earned. The earning of trust usually, in the course of life, is something that happens through people being 'honest' rather than 'safe'. An honest environment is an exciting and interesting place to be in, but like many exciting and interesting places, it is not a 'safe' place. 'Safe' places, with their rules, codes and sanctions, do not in fact promote free expression or much in the way of honesty, they become places in which 'safe' things are said. The safest thing I can say is what everyone expects me to say or that they will agree with, that is telling people what they already know or want to hear. Safe places are usually boring and boredom has always been the greatest taboo of youth.

That 'fuck off' moment

I was recently talking to a youth worker who complained that every time he approached a group of young men they told him to 'fuck off'. I asked him what he did when this happened and he told me 'I fuck off'. He explained this by saying that he was doing what the group wanted him to do (fuck off) and he saw that as 'giving them power'. But where does that get him or them? This didn't feel like a good use of council tax resources to me. Of course he could have asked 'Why are you talking to me like that?' Or he might have asked them why they wanted him to fuck off, or he might even have said 'Why should I fuck off? You fuck off' (although I have personally used versions of this last response in certain places at particular times, I wouldn't prescribe it to others as an initial riposte).

All of these would have at least prolonged his contact time with the group (even the latter response would have done this a bit) and offered a potential start of an association rather than a definite end. But I guess, in the last analysis, everyone stayed 'safe' and, as is the way with safety, in the same place where they started out from. It might be seen as going around in circles but no one even began the circle; this was something less than standing still. Something lived for a moment and died.

We begin, as people working with young people, with the intention of being part of an enterprise that teaches each other about 'us', and in that process we will learn a definite set of responses that can be related to most groups (although certainly in different ways) and that will be useful to you as people involved with others in your day to day work . . . Call the RAC!

- Regard
- Accompaniment
- Consideration

This can be translated in one-to-one situations but also in on-going collective (group) encounters.

Regard

A lot of time in our line of work is spent talking about 'respect', how people are 'entitled' to it, for example, and that we should make sure we 'give it' and so on. But respect is something, like trust, that has to be earned. I don't think I can just walk into a room and be trusted. Anyone who meets someone for the first time and just trusts them is either very naive or in need of psychiatric help.

In the run of things we tend to take time to learn if someone warrants, deserves or will value our trust. Like trust, respect cannot be front loaded. For all you know I might be a liar, a thief or a mass murderer, if you just 'give' me (and everyone else you meet) your respect in some random way, without any knowledge of me at all, what is that respect worth? What value does it have?

However, because we are professionals, paid and trusted to do the work we do with young people (I take it as read that we expect volunteers to act professionally) we do have certain duties and responsibilities that come with those considerations. This means that I don't treat the people I work with in exactly the same way as I would someone trying to sell me double glazing over the phone at 3am in the morning. Neither do I react to my wife or my father or my son in the same way as I would a person for whom I have a professional duty of care and who I am contracted (through my job description and so on) to work with, keeping the aims and objectives of the organisation I work for in mind.

If I do treat people I work with in the same way as I would everyone else it begs the question 'what is it I'm being paid for?' (or, as a volunteer, what or who am I doing this work for?) What special skills am I making use of in my work?

Me +

'I'm just being me' is an often heard cry (à la Big Brother) but to be given the care of others requires 'Me+'. If it doesn't my organisation could employ anyone and forget job descriptions and tell them 'just be yourself'. I was recently working with a young man (let's call him Fred) who had been asked to leave an employment placement after only two days. It seems Fred's dismissal followed a manager at the placement providing a box of chocolates for staff on the occasion of his birthday. Fred had made his way to the canteen to collect what he saw as his share of the gift only to find that all the confectionary had been devoured. That same day a long-term employee told Fred that she had eaten four of the chocolates. Fred's response was sincere and immediate; 'You fat cow!' He complained to me that he was basically 'sacked' for 'being honest' and 'speaking his mind'; for 'being himself'.

Apart from appearing to be unaware that his response was basically rude and insulting (even though he felt the 'fat cow' had 'deserved' his rebuke) what Fred did not understand fully was that he was in post to achieve the aims and objectives of the company he was working for, not to enjoy chocolates. He had no divine organisational 'right' to the chocolates and so no official grounds to insult someone about the same. As someone employed to work with young people, one's actions are similarly led by organisational agenda, and we are expected, at least to some extent, to comply with an 'organisational frame of reference'. This is a set of attitudes and values that are expected or even demanded of me by my employer; (Me+). 'Me' told to 'fuck off' will fuck off; 'Me+' being told to 'fuck off', as a model of a questioning person, with democratic principles, who doesn't want to become an example of how to successfully bully someone, might (but not immediately) 'fuck off' but I will not necessarily fuck off at all.

Whatever job you do in the field of care and/or education with young people, you are required to carry out certain tasks, things that ask more of you than just being who ever you perceive yourself to be.

Below is a short list of things that we do with those we work with which I'm sure you might add to. We:

- Attend to and care for them (which does not mean we just do what they tell us to do).
- Observe them.
- Record their activity.
- Value their contributions (we may openly agree or disagree with what they say or do).
- Are concerned about their well being etc.
- Are heedful of (listen to, watch) them (which might mean reacting in a way they might not expect).

This list is relevant right across the caring professions. A nurse might not respect a patient, but they must, to remain professional, care for their health needs (and sometimes tell them things they might not want to hear). A teacher might not trust a pupil, but given their employment and professional position they must seek to provide for their educational needs. A Me+ is required, because being 'just myself' might choose to simply walk away from people I do not trust, like or respect. In short, we 'respond', give 'regard' to those we work with – the '+' is the regard.

Esteeming in

The word 'regard' has its root in the idea of 'taking a second look' (re-gard). This is much more immediate than 'respect', the etymology of which indicates taking a more long-term (historical) inspection of the person or thing re-spected. When you regard a person, you are making more of an 'estimation' than an examination; you are, it might be said, holding them in 'esteem' (as you are seeing them worthy of your estimation). A lot of concern in our work is about the alleged 'low self-esteem' of some of those we work with (although it seems for many youth workers, nurses, police officers the super high-esteem [arrogance] of many young people seems to be more of a social problem). But you just can't go out and get some esteem. It takes at least two people to generate this (one person being held in esteem and another holding the other in esteem). The first indication that one is 'worthy' of esteem is the understanding that you are being regarded. If I am regarded it provides me with the basic building block of care; it is a confirmation of existence (I get more than one look, I become a person estimable of needing more than a cursory glance). At the same time, as I regard another and they respond to that regard, my own effect on another person is confirmed and that literally confirms me – it denotes my existence has been registered. Regard is therefore a mutually confirming activity that literally boosts esteem.

Attentive to attention

I often hear people say things like 'he only did it to get attention' or 'she's attention seeking'. The antidote to this are usually formulas that are designed to show people that their bid for attention has failed. 'Well, I just ignored him' or 'I showed her that her tantrum didn't pay off . . . I wasn't going to give her what she wanted', 'I was not going to give in to his demands'.

The consequence of this often goes one of two ways:

1. The ignored person walks away having been ignored in the search of some confirmation of their existence elsewhere.
2. The ignored person 'ups the anti' with an even greater performance because they need this confirmation 'here and now'.

A few years ago a person told me about a dinner party that she and her husband had attended. The hosts were telling their guests that their baby girl had for much of the first several months of her short life spent the best part of the night time crying. Having checked out the child's health with their GP, and finding no physical reason for the distress, a neighbour had advised the parents to ignore their child's 'grizzling' as she was clearly 'just seeking attention'. The parents tried this 'tactic' out. After a week or so the crying died down and eventually nights were quiet.

The dinner party was a great success and went undisturbed by the baby's tears. Before leaving, the parents took their two guests into the baby's room to take a look at her. The proud moment was spoilt as the four self-congratulatory adults saw that the baby was crying silently. Pain is still pain even if it is silenced by non-response, by not being regarded.

It surprises me that when someone is actually contracted to work with people and those people ask for the worker's attention, although perhaps not in the way that is easily understood or that is difficult to deal with, that it is felt reasonable to deny this request to be 'regarded', thus signalling to the attention seeker that they need to turn up the volume or piss off and annoy someone else (who may not be contracted or qualified to work with them).

Now this is not saying that we put up with anything that is thrown our way, rudeness (being called a 'fat cow' or being told to 'fuck off') or violence, we are not dustbins for people's psychological rubbish, but from long experience (my own and others) of such situations, I have found that the giving of regard actually can turn what seemed like rubbish into gold. Even given seemingly unreasonable demands one can still find ways of saying, 'I see you', 'I hear you – but it is not possible for me to work with you in this state of mind'. This is a rational and reasonable regard that actually invites a rational and reasonable response. That I might not get that is neither here nor there. I have retained own integrity, that is, I have not given up my responsibility, I have kept focused on my role and I have given a fair and clear message. At the same time I have not committed to any kind of retreat or disregard. I remain professional and I set out my requirements for my practice. I expect regard and I make my expectations completely overt.

This is not a prescription for you. I'm not offering a 'cure-all' here. It is no more than an example for you to consider (we will have more to say about that later). It is your 'judgement' that will give you 'your' response in any given situation (judgment is opinion mediated by evidence). But whatever your response, if it is delivered with the value of a regarding person, you have done your job and in one way or another you will see the fruits of that.

Totem of regard

Regard is primal to any association between people. Regard is what connects us, disregard disconnects us. The act of regard is a very straightforward and fundamental form of union between any living things. Regard is what keeps us alive and confirms to us that we are not dead and that we mean something.

A bus stop near where I work is regularly vandalised. I have seen it take many shapes after this 'attention'. In certain conditions the way the metal is curved by the 'vandals', together with the way the light catches the crystals of shattered shatter-proof glass, is quite striking; sometimes, if you look long enough (waiting for the rare passing of a bus), the effect is quite beautiful, as conditions (rain, night, headlights) create alternating shadow and reflection.

The bus stop is usually repaired pretty quickly, but sooner rather than later it is once more transformed to reflect anger or frustration or whatever the motivation is that converts this mundane shelter into a vague statement about the urban condition (art?). A totem of regard to being disregarded.

This is a very primitive exchange of regard; attention receiving attention; a mutual if messy encounter whose consistency seems to indicate satisfaction (at least by one party). This is of course not what bus shelters are for and I am not putting forward a charter for vandalism here. That the bus shelter is used in this way indicates a need; something is 'missing' in the area the bus stop 'serves'.

In the end, people have the power to make us regard them. If you think about it, disregard, the attempt to ignore someone, is a very attacking form of regard that in effect provokes a heightened form of aggression – the trick seems to be not to get to this point.

Accompaniment

Accompaniment is a means through which one might become more attuned to one's interaction with those we work with, for and among. It is a process encounter that arises out of mutual regard.

Friendly friendliness

Despite the popular adherence to the notion of 'befriending' we are not our client's friends. To be a client's friend means that they would no longer be a client and as such is by definition inappropriate – we are not employed to work with our friends and not everyone can be my friend – if they could then friendship would mean very little.

At the same time friendship requires more of all parties involved than is apt in a professional association, it also prevents as much as it facilitates. Friendships have the capacity to 'lead to other things' whereas professional relationships have definite boundaries. While these parameters might exceptionally be broken, if we are to operate effectively, according to organisational and policy guidelines, they cannot be breeched in an ad hoc or liberal way. But this does not stop us being 'friendly' towards those we work with. I can certainly extend friendliness to mostly anyone in the first instance.

I have often heard it said in youth work that 'you don't have to like someone to work with them'. This may well be true, but it surely makes life a little more bearable if you like those you have to spend most of your day with, and it's also no bad thing if they like you, too. The idea of spending the entirety of your working life with a good proportion of the people you don't like, and who don't like you, sounds like hell. That said, it probably makes sense to do what we can to like people and do our best to be liked. Why wouldn't we? It takes just as much effort to do the opposite.

Statements like, 'If you like it or not' and the more disturbing 'I don't care if you don't like me' coming from those employed to work with people to achieve their potential, to me never feel as if they get folk very far in terms of achieving professional ends (or non-professional ends). Indeed, if you really don't care at all what people think about you that could be seen as congruent with the psychic outlook of Narcissistic Personality Disorder. Millwall football fans have a mantra; 'Nobody likes us and we don't care'. This comes across as a quite powerful negative statement (and I guess this is meant). Its force comes from its dismissive quality and one can see the attraction in this as a defence; it has a great deal of potential for keeping people out. But it is a statement that isolates and reeks of a type of desperation; an almost autistic response that implies a sort of collective and purposeful loneliness.

Companionship

Accompaniment, being actively with a companion (companionship) is a 'friendly' attitude that exists to generate an atmosphere of 'associative activity'. It is a place wherein regard is given but also expected on a mutual basis. With this foundation in place a situation can be fostered in which trust in that 'field effect' that exists between two people, can evolve and be exchanged as it is earned or justified.

In accompaniment we work to build our awareness of the presence of our companion (we build companionship). As our companion shares their dreams, struggles, triumphs, disappointments, joys and fears, they express their deepest and wisest source of their potential.

When examining the character of accompaniment, for analysis sake, I call the professional the 'accompanist' and the client the 'companion'. In practice both (all) those involved in accompaniment are companions in that they 'travel' together. They are also both accompanists, but they constantly change places in time as each directs the journey in turn, but in the main the companion (client) finds the path, so by and large the professional is the accompanist – but this is not a rule as all journeys are unique and as such start and conclude differently.

As a professional accompanist, you work with your companion to notice, savour and respond to the world, but more than this you are open to them introducing aspects of their perception to you (and of you). This, of course, can only happen if you do the same in return. People are much more likely to tell you what they think (on a consistent basis) if you tell them what you think. So it is more about how 'we' see things, than how 'you' see things. This exchange of ideas and perceptions is what Marx called the 'Dialectic' – a fusion of perceptions.

Dialectic – heard and seen

Some time ago I accompanied a group of young deaf people on a trip to the theatre to see a comedy play. We were sitting front of house so that the group could lip read. Throughout the performance the group were 'chatting' (using sign language) and were laughing in the 'wrong' places (there were moments when they laughed while the rest of the audience were not laughing and failed to laugh when everyone else in the theatre was laughing). I found this intriguing and became more interested in their response than the play itself (such is the cost of regard).

As we left the theatre I was approached by a person who told me she was the theatre manager. She wanted to 'apologise' because the theatre did not have a 'loop system' and told me that next time we came there would be one in place. She was sorry that the lack of a loop had 'spoilt' the group's enjoyment of the play and that next time they would enjoy it 'better'.

I was a little taken aback because the group had seemingly enjoyed the play. They confirmed this on our way home, generally agreeing the trip had been 'fun'. But I was curious about what they had found funny in the play, the bits that had apparently gone over the heads of the rest of the audience. They explained how they had seen things. In turn they asked me about the things I had laughed at which they had not responded to. I soon began to see that while they were conscious of being 'deaf' to some of the humour, that I had not been aware how much my hearing had 'blinded' me to what was going on. Our trip home was in fact a dialectical rebuilding of the play, a merging of consciousness and understanding that overall provided a far richer appreciation of our experience than we might otherwise have had.

Since that experience I have often asked myself if the theatre manager's 'loop system' would have effectively prevented the mutual exploration I had experienced with the group. It would certainly have created something different again (better or worse it is impossible to say). But this dialectic (for Marx) is the source of human change and invention; it is the means by which 'I' move on from where 'I' am to where 'we' are.

Fuzzy dialogue

Some academics in the 'people professions' have seemingly spent lifetimes writing of the virtues of 'dialogue', but the notion suggests little more than 'chat' or 'gossip'. In itself it is no bad thing, but the direction or trajectory of dialogue is 'fuzzy' – it does not, of necessity, lead anywhere in particular. It feels 'liberal' but is more realistically what goes on in intellectual ghettos (psychic and physical ghettos). The minimal demand of dialogue tends to be the exchange of what people already know or the pooling of ignorance. It may graduate to dialectic, but this is neither a conscious nor a purposeful effort, and if it happens at all it is by accident (in this event what can happen with the outcome is limited). Dialectic is something up the evolutionary scale relative to dialogue and is consciously directed at questioning and exploration rather than just being talk that is an end in itself – dialectic is purposeful and critical and it seeks outcomes in an overt and sustained manner. As such it is appropriate to the professional task in a manner that dialogue just is not:

- Dialectic is an organic yet purposeful response and a professional tool.
- Dialogue is an inadequate response to the professional purpose.

Authentic listening

As an accompanist one listens and responds in an 'authentic' way. This is something a bit more than honesty – we can't always be totally honest with those we work with and although we can work towards that point, honesty is sometimes, in some places with some people a very blunt instrument. If you honestly think that someone is a 'loser' or a 'liar' (or a 'fat cow') it is a usually a very subjective point of view and often based on very little knowledge of the person. Authenticity is akin to the expression of professional judgement in that it is opinion based on evidence. For all this, in accompaniment the aim of those involved is to create an environment wherein issues and feelings can be explored, examined, scrutinised and managed in a genuine manner.

Pretend relationships

Accompaniment is always aimed at generating firstly a connection and then a union between people. But we do not seek a 'relationship'. Our work is dominated by the expressions like 'professional relationship', and we are told that we need to build 'relationships' with young people. But the connection we have with those we work with, if looked at as a relationship, comes over as very one-sided. It is the professional that usually inaugurates the so-called relationship (in one way or another) if only by being employed to 'be there'. Even if one is a volunteer, there is a need to work within organisational codes of practice and greater policy parameters. It is also the case that no matter how the situation is going, the professional can usually call an end to any interaction almost immediately. Professionals leave jobs; they change employment and go on holiday (without the client). It is hard to think of any 'relationship' that is so one sided.

We are also (especially in much of the literature on informal education and youth work) told to 'use' relationships for what are often covert ends (the aims of an individual professional or an organisation, and we need to work within local and national guidelines of 'best practice'). This purposeful 'using' of relationships seems to me at least, unethical and not a way I would personally like to be treated.

This aside, a relationship requires a certain type of commitment on both (or all) sides. Without this, one does not have a relationship. I think this is why so many clients tend to view what they have with professionals as something inauthentic. 'On the tin' it says that these people 'care' about me, that they will 'help' and 'support' me and that they claim to have a relationship with me. Yet I know they won't be there on a Sunday afternoon, they won't have me round to dinner, they won't write to me when they leave the job and they wouldn't have much to do with me if they weren't paid to. If we are in relationship with our clients it sometimes feels a bit like prostitution; it is something of a 'pretend relationship'.

Association

Perhaps a more valid way of talking and thinking about our interaction with clients is to understand it as association. This suggests the 'light formality' and a convivial yet structured nature that fits with what we need to be doing in our professional role. Unlike friendship, our connection with those we work with requires us to 'do' prescribed things – we have an official brief that does not really exist in the ideal of friendship or relationship. We comply with all sorts of rules and regulations, codes and conventions that do not apply in 'relationships'. Yes, we can call what we have with our client in the professional situation a 'low level relationship' but how 'low' do you want to go? Perhaps a high level association is preferable to a low level relationship?

In accompaniment we build a useful association with those we work with (our companions). It is pragmatic and although we are on a journey that brings up all sorts of challenges, altercations and alterations to plans, at any point, all those involved should have some clear boundaries and shared goals. Although we might be friendly, we do not befriend or pretend by suggestion or implication that we are 'friends' – we make it clear what we are about and what the nature of the association is.

The trajectory of the journey we accompany our companions on is towards them realising their potential and as such their wholeness. Its compass is the continued development of awareness and the task can be relatively straightforwardly passed on between professionals within a caring network of association. That happens not somewhere 'outside' the companions but within the accompaniment.

In accompaniment the flowering of awareness is a mutual thing. As I become more aware of my companions and their journey so it provides a field effect that implicates all those involved in the accompaniment – the process of awareness necessarily works all ways. Our map emerges out of this mutually expanding awareness and our atlas is constantly added to in terms of detail by the continuing advance of association from connection to union between accompanist and companion.

Collaboration – active of non-therapy

Accompaniment is not a therapy. In youth work, and the supervision of youth work, lots of people seem to think, or act as if they are involved in, some form of therapy and/or counselling. You might be qualified to do this, most people aren't and in the main we do not tell the folk we work with that's what we are going to do with them. The work of accompaniment is much more collaborative than the conventional therapeutic interaction. It seeks no cures and does not assume any deficits like 'neuroses', attention deficit disorder or lack of self-esteem. Because, as a companion, I am not geared to starting out with an idea that my companion 'lacks' something, I do not perceive them as a person in need of 'help', cure or 'support'. They may benefit (like most of us) from someone working with them to understand what it is they want to get out of life or any given situation, someone ready and willing to walk alongside them in search of increased awareness – a colleague of mine called herself 'a life detective' – but she was a friend of David Simon – which on consideration might be a useful as a technical source (see Simon, 1993). However, as my companion has expectations of me, I too have expectations of them. If there is any 'helping' to be done or any need of 'support', it is likely to be the accompanist who will need it, as it is their job to look to understand the companion (in the first instance) and the only person that can assist me with that is my companion.

Accompanist – Association – Companion

Accompaniment
= Being actively with a companion, in companionship
= A 'friendly' setting that exists to generate an atmosphere of 'associative activity'.
Companionship
Collaboration
Friendliness

Regard given and expected on a mutual basis

Trust exchanged as it is earned

'Dialectic'

Purposeful and Critical

Authentic listening and response

Association

Finding and responding

In short, accompaniment is concerned with 'finding' and 'responding' more than helping and supporting. This may involve a certain amount of 'problem solving' but this is necessary led most of the time by my companion (as we are not on the journey to sort out my problems). In accompaniment the professional is much more a follower than a director – we become 'interactive shadows'. But we are not slaves. We own our own individual agenda (the terms on which the association is based) and these are constantly made overt and if necessary reiterated assertively. This clears a path for our companion in association to take advantage of our followership and look within themselves for leadership skills. The accompanist might point out some of these leadership abilities as the accompaniment continues, not because the companion is seen as ignorant of them but because of the need to acknowledge their leadership and the followership of the accompanist and also giving regard. The accompanist might also, from time to time, 'take a lead' but only with continuing the journey of discovery in mind; the accompanist's intervals of leading are designed not to make them the leader but to stimulate the leadership qualities of the companion or just to give them a bit of a rest (this in effect restates the collaborative nature of accompaniment). The shadow never tries to take over the person – however the 'colonialisation nightmare' is what many professionals play out with their clients, which of course alienates the person who is supposed to be getting the benefit of the encounter.

In many ways, the pivotal point in whether you are able to accompany someone is your own attitudes. In this very active form of 'being with' the accompanist needs to remain 'alive' and constantly 'functioning'. They are a follower and a servant (they work more 'for' than 'with' or 'on' a person) but this is not all the accompanist is. This subtle and generous 'Sherpa' role is energy sapping and you have to acclimatise to it. It is a highly vigorous role that draws on one's focused integrity.

If you see someone as relatively incapable or reliant or dependent, it is likely that you will work 'with' or 'on' them, albeit unconsciously, to fulfil this expectation (maybe this need) that you have. But if you perceive your companion as a whole being, with all the capacities necessary to move into the world, someone who (like most of us) requires expectations in order that they might do something; a person who not only has the potential to make demands but also the need to respond to the demands of others, then there is a good chance that both you and your companion are in for an interesting if challenging (and at times not altogether 'safe') journey.

Deficit presumptions

This can be an amazing experience for the accompanist. I have a friend who works with street children in an East African city. He is always full of inspiring tales about those he works among. Some of these people are as young as five and six, but his admiration for their inventiveness and ability is massively refreshing. For example, 11-year-old Henry has built his own place to live and he has developed a newspaper-selling business. He has generated a co-operative with 12 other children and has done deals with local food sellers to make sure his workers are fed night and morning. This is just one of many accounts about how young people develop their potential in the face of seemingly impossible odds, how they work together and find a way. It is so different from the depressing stories that I hear from many working with young people in the so called developed world, that often start out from a statement like 'I'm working with a young man with learning difficulties'. I can't help but ask myself, 'Learning for what? About what? Who has decided what is to be learnt, when and how the 'learning' happens? Difficulties relative to what and who? Did he make this judgment about his learning or was it a sentence passed on him by an assuming professional? Who is qualified make this deficit prognosis? On what criteria has this claim been based?' Unfortunately, in the main, such questions go unasked and discussion continues as if the young man's 'learning difficulties' were a fact rather than the product of a prejudicial, subjective, partial and largely uninformed set of assumptions.

Patience is needed. Many of those we work with have long been treated as if they are in deficit. Young people are seen as almost naturally lacking experience (and/or something else) although I know many 50 year olds who are a lot less experienced than some 15 year olds I have known. At the same time we have almost been trained to see those we work with in deficit (when we were their age we were probably treated in much the same way in terms of being seen as lacking) – many people come into our line of work because they see themselves as wanting or needing to 'help' or 'support' others, making them 'better' (as if they were ill!). These folk are bound for disappointing, relatively unfulfilling careers. Medicine might have been a more suitable route?

Connection to union

To move into accompaniment takes diligence on our part and a preparedness to wait while the nature of the association between you and your companion is digested by you both as it matures from connection into union. This is our 'professionalism' and our discipline. In turn this requires a sort of trust or confidence (professional confidence) both in yourself and what might be called human nature. Again this is a big ask, because few of us trust ourselves or others this much and it is a real test of confidence (self esteem) in what you are looking to do. Giving up on it and just doing things 'to' people is a much easier option and that route does make you look and feel busy. However, sticking with the process of remaining attentive to the direction of your companion and maintaining a benign yet definite presence does pay dividends both to your companion and yourself. In its best incarnation these journeys become epiphanies, as those involved move from knowledge to understanding, to insight, to awareness, to revelation.

In accompaniment, it is important for there to be a mutual sense of the rightness (right-wayness, righteousness) which is different to 'correctness' of the association and a concern for authentic, clear communication and a reverence for the unique way my companion is working to become what they need to be. They might not be very practiced at expressing themselves, or they might be extremely well practiced in saying what they want to, but it is just that you can't recognise or appreciate it (the latter is probably more often the case than the former). Coupled with this is a mutual dependence (interdependence) upon each other, or you might say on the association.

The conduit of understanding

Human specifics of age, gender, religion, culture and so forth, assume more importance at one time in a person's life than at another. But basically it is only necessary that those in association experience the kind of 'fitness' that allows them to be free for their common purpose together without undue attention to the association itself – the association is the means, the conduit of understanding and awareness – it exists to promote authentic expressions and exploration – it is not a friendship or a love affair as all human encounters it has definite practical purposes, aims and objectives that might alter and/or take time to become obvious. However, essential association takes place on a life journey and is a process of discovery.

Invitation not intervention

It is paramount that you, as a professional companion in accompaniment are responding to an invitation or permission from your companion to participate in their journey, although this might not always be readily recognisable (the first response you get might be 'fuck off') and that together you give that path a direction. As an accompanist you are not intervening – it is not an incursion and it is not invasive, as such you will need to commit to a constant awareness of the nature of the association that is premised on the gifts and skills of your companion and the finding of their potential through means appropriate to her or his particular wants via invitation, summons, incitement or ignition.

The primary responsibilities of the accompanist are regard for the companion, consideration of their wants and the way you are working 'for' them. This assumes that the accompanist is taking seriously his/her role in association and giving attention to both what they are and more particularly what they are not (counsellor, lover, sibling, therapist, friend, parent etc.). Further, as a means of accountability, keeping a firm hold on role and personal growth, accompanists build on their ability via consideration with others committed to accompaniment (this might be thought of as a chain of accompaniment).

Accompanists walk alongside others on their life journey. This will almost certainly never be a life long commitment and we probably benefit from having many different accompanists in the course of our existence. Sometimes we might even benefit from travelling alone and at points we may have to. But the goodbye should always be expressed by people who are better informed, more aware and more confident than when they said hello. In the last analysis they will need less encouragement, because they will not have a great lack of courage; they will not need empowering because they will understand that they have authority over themselves and that they are able to use it, so taking control over their lives. They will also not need anyone to enable them because they will not see themselves as 'dis-abled'.

Oceans of life

In association the true director is the life lived. We respond to it, accommodate it and as such take some control of our destiny. We come to realise that while we sail on a rough social sea, we are not corks to be tossed about by the elements in the hope that we will be picked up by some kind yet dominant force. We find that we have a rudder and sails or even outboard motors and engines. We make charts and a compass and we find our own way across the oceans of life – if we are lucky we do this in the good company of a discerning listener, who recognises our human potential, who responds to our expectations with expectations of us so we can become responding persons and not just someone who gets responses. I am affirmed and affirm in turn . . . my affirmation of my companion is my power working and I feel it.

Accompaniment takes us to the source of humanity's yearning for deeper meaning and the search for purpose in our lives. It is a generous association that relies for its life on both give and take. It accepts rather than tolerates, it embraces more than it engulfs and in the end it concludes as it began; with a departing.

Consideration

In the 'people professions', including nursing, youth work, social work and policing, practitioners are encouraged to 'reflect' on their practice and the term, the 'reflective practitioner' has become a widely used kite mark across these professions. This reflective practice is often undertaken with what is effectively the tutelage of more experienced peers, mentors or supervisors and involves looking back on what has been done in a critical manner, essentially to imagine how whatever was done might have been done better or more effectively. On the rare occasions when things, 'on reflection', have gone as well as possible, say we hired a bouncy castle for a fund raising event and made loads of money, the idea is that we apply a similar strategy at our next fund raising event. However, for the most part, we are encouraged to reflect on how to make our practice stronger by seeking out/identifying our errors, flaws, mistakes, miscalculations etc. As such reflective practice involves developing imaginary responses to past activity, the results of which might be called upon in the future if anything occurs like what has occurred before.

The three main problems with this process are:

1. It makes the jump that things will happen like they have happened before.
2. It works on the principle that we 'learn from our mistakes'.
3. Reflection mirrors and distorts reality, it does not replicate it.

The dangers of seeing a unique event that is happening in the present as being similar or the same as one that has happened in the past are easily imagined.

The last time we hired a bouncy castle it was a lovely day. It was a Sunday in June. It was a novelty (as we had never hired a bouncy castle before). This time the event is taking place on a Saturday in August.

Three months ago the local jam factory laid off 250 workers for an indefinite period.

According to the weather forecast it is going to be a showery day.

In July a bouncy castle that was being used at a fete in Penge made the news when it was punctured and carried four pensioners who were aboard at the time into the lake at Crystal Palace.

Is our bouncy castle going to get the same response as it did the first time round?

As far as 'learning from our mistakes' goes, the evidence from most people's lives is that we tend to make the same mistakes over and over again. What we seem to learn from our mistakes is that they weren't mistakes at all, just misfortunes; the idea was right but the timing was wrong (the recent credit crunch is a fine macro-economic example of this human propensity). Hence at another time the same strategy (which I'm very attached to, otherwise I wouldn't have followed it in the first place) will work! It's not a problem with application, its bad luck, fate, destiny . . . I recall one awful mistake being explained when someone remembered 'We forgot to pray!'

This being the case, I'm not a great fan of reflective practice. It is far too passive for me to be comfortable with – almost like an accident waiting to happen. The main problem with it is that has the seeds of its own failure set within it; it sees the past as an accurate and reliable guide to the future (rather than what the past actually is – a reference). However, I have successfully used and seen others deploy the idea of applying 'disciplined consideration' of work.

Unlike reflection, consideration is set in the 'now'. It is centrally focused on 'concerns' that might arise from recorded practice, but also by 'conjecture' about possibilities. In that sense it takes a global 'considerate' view of events. For example, the tactic of 'befriending' is promoted in much of the literature and teaching surrounding youth work and related fields. In this, the professional takes on the guise of a 'friend' to the client. They might not identify themselves overtly as a friend and covertly, say in conversations with other professionals, they are likely to deny any friendship exists between themselves and the client, yet it is generally suggested that there is a 'relationship' and it is at least implied to the client that friendship is being offered. Reflection on this situation would generally be on the 'success' or otherwise of this situation in terms of relatively short term outcomes, perhaps if the client shows 'movement' or whatever over a given period – say six months of 'befriending' activity.

Disciplined consideration of this tactic (for that is what it is – a plan that in another incarnation might be called 'entrapment' or 'grooming') will look at the wider consequences both prior to and after any such strategy is carried out. In effect the role of 'befriender' will be 'problematised' as it is subjected to 'professional consideration'. A straightforward definition of the notion of professionalism is;

Taking responsibility for and dealing with the consequences of one's actions.

So, we would be looking at the whole meaning of 'befriending', including its morality, its ethical foundations, its professional pretensions, its effect on the client and the professional at the point of practice and in the future, including the potential (that comes with friendship) of collusion, secrecy (which is not the same as confidentiality) and other 'inappropriate' relations and commitments.

Consideration raises concerns. It includes careful deliberation about matters, uses **advisement** and calculation and the extension of 'secure kindness'. It involves thoughtfulness and sometimes **study.** It requires concentration and **attention.** It makes use of accompaniment, **heedfulness** and regard. It is solicitous in that it is bound by disciplined care and attention to detail. It is deferential to the client, seeks collaborative approval and acknowledges professional **accountability.**

Consideration includes **admiration** and **appreciation** of the client in that it holds them in **esteem** and seeks to **honour** their individuality and unique behaviour over time. It is not based on one person asking questions and another answering them (according to Will Hunting (1998) no equality exists in an interaction like this) – consideration is dialectical.

Consideration, being bound up with regard, authenticity and accompaniment, calls on the client for advice and guidance, but will also pass on judgements made about them as and when relevant and/or appropriate and will include the giving of advice and information about expectations – this is required at points to move thesis on to antithesis so away from ghetto thinking and create synthesis (a dialectic).

It seems to me that it is a war cry of the youth worker – that they 'never give advice'. In my work I probably hear this phrase more than any other. The reason for this is usually something like 'because it is unfair to impose my opinions to a young person'. Subjecting this to consideration it can be seen that it is a wonderful example of how the professional ego can delude someone into imagining themselves as having such power. The truth is that many things (if not most) that youth workers say to young people will be responded to by the young person doing the exact opposite (or merely ignoring them). The idea that as soon as I say something to a young person they will take it as gospel (because I am an 'adult') is another instance of the deficit model in action. It sees young people as basically simple, not capable of consideration, compliant and 'easily led' – as the coloniser saw the colonised in the era of Empire. The evidence of this being the case in terms of young people, more than any other group, I suggest is at best negligible.

Young people are the most disaffected of groups, discriminated against and subject to prejudice like this at every turn. They have less access to civil rights than any other group you care to name and all access to almost anything can only be had via adult intervention (adults have duties and responsibilities towards young people rather than young people having rights in their own right). They are an utterly colonised group. Why are we surprised when they 'rebel'? The problem is not that young people might rebel, the difficult question for those of us that talk of equality, justice and democracy is why we are not rebelling with them. I write this after much consideration.

As you can see, the problem for the professional is that consideration takes us outside the bounds of the usual limits of reflection. It drags us into the now and poses all sorts of questions about the future. Perhaps that's why its use as a disciplined means of professional analysis is, in the main, avoided. As this book concludes you might find it useful to consider this.

I have concluded this work with the above section as all the pages you have or might have read in this book have been written for your consideration. Not a word, not a chapter, has been built as a completed work. In the tradition that no work for an audience is finished until its audience has viewed it, the next phase is therefore the building, and it will be built (or not) in your practice with young people and the continuance and elaboration of the traditions of youth work; an independent and vibrant discipline that while it might deploy informal and community education techniques and theory, is not those pursuits. Youth work has a future, but it will be made only if there is the will to do it on the part of professionals and young people. And that is in your hands.

References

Hunting, W. (1998) Asin B00004CZNL. Walt Disney Studios.

Masson, J. (1989) *Against Therapy.* HarperCollins.

Ollman, B. (1993) *Dance of the Dialectic: Steps in Marx's Method.* University of Illinois Press.

Simon, D. (1993) *Homicide: a Year on the Killing Streets.* Simon Ivy Books.

Walt Disney Studios (1998) *Good Will Hunting.* dvd – Director: Gus Van Sant, Writers: Damon, M., Affleck, B. Producers: Bob Weinstein, Chris Moore, Harvey Weinstein, Jonathan Gordon, Kevin Smith.

Conclusion

By Zuber Ahmed

Zuber was born, and grew up, in the East End of London. Both his parents are from Bangladesh. Like many of us in the profession, as a young person, he didn't set out to be a youth and community worker, but started out doing part-time youth work in his case while studying business and finance, he had intended to become an accountant.

Although he understood accountancy would be financially more rewarding, his part time work, in his own words 'put me in touch with some of the basic themes of my life, that people matter and that love and our time are all we have to offer each other that means anything'. So he went to college and completed the Foundation Certificate in Youth Work with the YMCA George Williams College and went on to gain a BA Hons degree at the same institution. He recalls:

> Everything that I read, listened to and everything I did made me stop and think. It helped me to explore issues in a different way and I worked my way to some conclusions.

Zuber has worked in several voluntary youth and community organisations in a range of settings, from detached youth work to conventional youth club environments. He has also been involved with several international youth programmes. This he says has afforded him the opportunity to experience and appreciate how diverse youth and community work actually is. It is a career he feels passionately about. He is presently employed by Tower Hamlets Youth Service, as a Senior Youth Worker, managing a youth centre and a team of staff.

Zuber presents a summation of the ideas and positions introduced in previous chapters as a critical assessment of the nature and claims of informal education. He argues that current informal education settings and delivery can create methods which are coercive and oppressive, whilst at the same time serve to tighten state control and discipline over young people via education policy. He sees this process as part of a wider attempt to control people's behaviour.

He refers to 'The Matrix', trilogy of science-fiction-adventure films written and directed by the Wachowski brothers and produced by Joel Silver. Using the Matrix as an allegory, Zuber compares the computerised Matrix programme created by machines in the movies, with the 'programme' created by the state and its allied multinational corporations. Within this programme, the

values, skills and beliefs of one group of people (who might be thought of as colonisers), dominate traditional values, skills and beliefs of people and cultures.

During this exploration, the 'wall' referred to in Pink Floyd's 1979 rock opera, 'The Wall', written by bassist and then Pink Floyd lead songwriter, Roger Waters, will be explored as will the notion of 'empowerment' and the role of the state in our practice.

Damage control on thought control

The state control of education, together with the legal obligation of every individual to attend institutions tasked with the delivery of state education during the most determining years of life, means that in its every incarnation education becomes a conduit to forward state aims; it is, as such, a tool for political control and manipulation – and can be thought of as an instrument used to police thoughts of the society. This sounds a bit dramatic, but the very influence education has over defining what is right and wrong and the training of young people to take up roles in society makes it an arena that is tactically sensitive and as such one government might be loath to step back from because of its potential, alongside the media, as a means of indoctrination and a channel for the delivery of propaganda.

In Britain every child passes through what is practically the same indoctrination process – the 'knowledge' they acquire is of the same 'official history', allegiance to the same 'civic virtues' are promoted while value is given to obedience and loyalty to the state. In this atmosphere it becomes extremely difficult for the teacher or the individual student to see beyond the straightjacket of the ideology and values the political authorities wish to imprint upon the population under its jurisdiction.

In this environment what alternatives there might be to the existing social system are depicted as anachronistic or simply irredeemably flawed. Hence critique of the current social form is so often met with the question 'So what alternatives are there?' the helplessness of which is punctuated by the usual follow-up statement 'Communism didn't work!' Likewise ideas of Theocracy are compared to aspects of current brutal and repressive autocratic regimes. However, if one fails to be presented with possible alternatives how can one envisage what an alternative might be?

For the Communist Russians of the early 20th century (in reality a form of severe, centralised bureaucracy) it was the class struggle and obedience to the Party and Comrade Stalin; for the Fascists, it was worship of the nation state and deference to the El Duce; for the Nazis, it was race purity and obedience to the Fuhrer. The content has varied, but the form has remained the same; as in Orwell's 'Nineteen-Eighty-Four' 'Resistance is useless', a situation which stymies the potential to create anything new. Through the institution of compulsory state education, the child is to be moulded like wax into the shape desired by the state by those entrusted to enter its elite cadre of professional educators.

Donaldo Macedo begins his introduction to *Chomsky on Miseducation* (2000) by describing the paradoxical tensions that compulsory education in so-called free and open societies face today. On one hand, the education of children and young people is charged with the responsibility of passing on the virtues of democracy and on the other this education is complicit with – indeed it plays a primary role in the construction of, the inherent hypocrisy of contemporary democracies. He states:

> *Because they don't teach the truth about the world, schools have to rely on beating students over the head with propaganda about democracy.*

Nowhere is this form of 'democracy' more clear than in the recent education policy in Britain.

The tacit or 'hidden' curriculum of schools is made manifest in the questions that are not asked, the areas of life that are ignored and the implicit assumptions about people and society that remain unexamined. This results in a situation wherein students rarely have the opportunity to think critically about the world. In fact, the function of educating the young:

> *. . . is to keep people from asking questions that matter about important issues that directly affect them and others.*
>
> Ibid.: 24

From the perspective of the state, the purpose of educating young people, is to teach what's right and wrong in terms of state definitions while engineering consumers (Illich, 1970:45) creating a 'new world religion' (the market). For Illich, economics takes what is best about humanity and deeply corrupts it. It turns care, love, neighbourliness, kindness, community – indeed, most of the deeply humane aspects of our life – into professional economic services. This attitude is confirmed in state education and other state funded projects to fulfil the overriding aim of the capitalist state, to ensure the nation has a *successful economy* (Foster, 2005: 2–5).

In *Deschooling Society* (1970) Illich maintained that that schooling perpetuates itself through a hidden curriculum. State controlled education cultivates a perpetual dissatisfaction in children; there is always 'something' better, 'something' to want, 'something' to gain (this 'something' could be taken literally as a material object) or figuratively (a nameless, faceless emptiness or longing). People are indoctrinated to believe that skills are valuable and reliable only if they are the result of formal education or forms of certification or accreditation (Illich, 1970: 91). This consumerism and dissatisfaction are part of what Illich named the 'hidden curriculum' in State education – the information, attitudes, goals, values, etc., inculcated in children via the processes of what is called 'education'.

Illich demonstrates that the education system in Western Society is a propaganda machine designed to serve the interests and agendas of the dominant strata of society – those in receipt of the profits of consumerism and their political allies/supporters. The implementation of state policy and laws, for example, compulsory education, suggest that children and parents are unable/incapable of making the 'right' decision, i.e., the decision to take up education. In our society the decision to take part in education is, at least up to the age of 18, not an individual choice. The rhetoric about choice in education is made nonsense by the fact that as far as the education of our children is concerned we follow the orders dictated to us by authorities or risk the punishment of the law. What is called compulsion is actually coercion and it can be enforced via state sanctioned violence (violation of freedom for instance). The potential for parents and children to take responsibility for their own education and their autonomy to make decisions about their own learning is usurped by the state.

The above is not suggesting that education should never be organised, or approached in holistic and diverse ways. The questions being posed are:

- Who is doing the organising?
- For whom?
- How?
- To what ends?
- What space is there for disorganising and re-organising?

Youth workers in both the state and voluntary sectors, like teachers, are charged with the delivery of government policy and agenda. The desire of the state to promote its objectives through national policies influences the nature and direction of our practice. We are increasingly directed by senior staff to comply with local authority aims. These, together with much of the alternative funding streams, via trusts and quangos, reflect or adhere to government policy and directives.

Social policy and legislation is premised on a set of assertions about what is 'good' or what is 'right' for society. This codifies, defines, regulates and restricts what can be delivered to service users but it also characterises the nature of recipients of these services. For example, in 2002 the Department of Education and Skills document entitled 'Transforming Youth Work: Resourcing Excellent Youth Services' (REYS, 2002: 16) sets out clear targets for local authorities in terms of their provisions to young people:

> . . . of the 25 per cent reached in the 13–19 target population, 60 per cent to undergo personal and social development which results in an accredited outcome.

This has some powerful implications for young people in terms of how society views them; it gives an impression that young people are somehow deficient and not fully human. They are thought to come to us underdeveloped personally and socially. While there is no concrete evidence to support this assumption, if one is to access the resources effectively attached to this policy, one must be seen to comply with the identity it describes as its potential beneficiaries.

At the same time, the policy immediately places young people in a position of a thing (a target – which is further dehumanising). At the same time the youth worker is seen as being in a position of authority; they are the person who acts on/treats the underdeveloped young person via assessment for accreditation.

One of the difficulties with defining youth work in such narrow terms is that it excludes groups and communities that are not readily conscripted to such definitions that allow relatively unrestricted access to resources. If young people want to access youth services, they must give up their self-determination and allow someone else to direct them by allowing the identification and assessment of their needs by someone else or at least according to standards they have had no part in creating. This is followed by building programmes to address their assessed need.

However, even when a young person chooses not to be accessed for youth provisions they may well nevertheless be approached and persuaded to be part of this process. This act of 'persuasion', which is effectively aimed at altering the behaviour of a potential recipient, is more or less an explicit form of manipulative indoctrination and a controlling mechanism that reinforces and reproduces forms of oppressive social hegemony. The process might involve low-level forms of bribery (rewards in kind) vague threats (of what and might not happen if they continue to refuse to be part of the programme) or, especially if their peers have been conscripted, a level of social isolation.

How can youth workers be said to be respectful of the self-determination of young people and their capacity to make free choices (as they frequently boast they do) if they indulge in such activity? For all this, the idea that young people are allowed to act without external compulsion to determine their own status or independence is made a contradiction in terms by the word 'allowed'; who is doing the 'allowing'? There is very little 'voluntary' about a service that in part distinguishes itself by way of the 'voluntary participation' of its users.

For most of us, in its best incarnation, education is about human development rather than merely a means of maximising human resources (what has been termed as and contracted to 'social capital'). To learn what is a 'good' learners need to identify for themselves what values they see as central to human growth and well being, and how such values are transmitted and distorted in the interests of those in authority. However, at present vast numbers of people are being subject to forms of more or less subtle coercion to take on values and perform tasks that advance certain groups in society while at the same time being directed to achieve ends demanded by dominant political and economic groups.

How can education be an authentically liberating experience unless it is relevant to the individual being educated first and foremost? How can it be relevant unless it includes opportunities for people to explore and understand their own historical, political and cultural position in relation to the wider context of their lives (see Freire, 1970)? By definition any progressive agenda would include . . . *freedom at the top of the curriculum* (Bremer, 1971: 29). If any of this does not pertain isn't it doubtful that what is going on is in fact education?

Liberation or social control?

Chomsky's analysis of state sponsored education is particularly relevant in light of the current assault of test-driven activity in youth work. For him indoctrination is necessary because state sanctioned and controlled education is for the most part intended to support the interests of dominant social groups, groups and individuals with authority and wealth. This is the root of the intensive testing and state regulation of what is taught in and interpreted as education. According to Chomsky one of the main lessons of education is that failure to support the interests of those with authority and wealth can threaten one's own advancement and even survival. The process which enforces values and maintains order is termed *social control* (Hoghughi, 1983: 26).

The Matrix (1999) provides an interesting perspective that echoes aspects of social control in current society. Machines dominate the planet and create a computerised Matrix programme, which controls the minds of humans. People are led to believe they were living 'normal' lives. But in reality it is the Matrix that constructs that reality and it is designed to completely control humanity. As *Agent Smith*, an aspect of the Matrix that assumes human form, designed to keep order and avoid instability in the simulated reality (he does this in the first instance by way of persuasion – a sort of cyber generated informal educator) tells the history of the Matrix thus:

> . . . the first Matrix was designed to be a perfect human world. Where none suffered, where everyone would be happy. It was a disaster. No one would accept the programme.

Some people escape the Matrix and seek support from others who have already exited the Matrix, but the threat of the machine continues as it endeavours to return the renegades to the Matrix.

The Matrix might be likened to a racist society in as much as the machine regarded humans with disgust and contempt. In colonial society dominant groups (colonisers) demonstrated that they were only concerned for the well being of the colonised as efficient labour, seeing them as inferior. The colonisers, like the machines, were focused primarily on appropriating resources, generally by violent means, taking control of decision-making processes, educational and religious institutions. This effectively kept the colonised within the programme and, as Fanon points out, not fully aware of the extent to which the colonisers dominated their perceptions and attitudes. The Matrix is also a place wherein humans were expected to stay in the programme unaware that they were being supremely manipulated.

Following the US bombing of Afghanistan in 2001, the Bush Administration resurrected the hackneyed colonial notion that its military intervention was intended to save people from their oppressors – Muslim women were highlighted. As Laura Bush said, *The fight against terrorism is also a fight for the rights and dignity of women* (*The Independent*, 2006). That line was really intended for people in the US. However, in its own history it is evident that the US has preferred to support authoritarian leaders who systematically violate women's rights.

In youth work practice it is the dominant economic and political groups (the colonisers) that create policy premised on values and traditions that effectively continue and enhance the exploitation of target groups (the colonised). The education of which youth work is a part, primarily functions to produce a comparatively cheap, relatively adaptable, compliant work force. However, this situation is camouflaged by the insistence that the measures included in policy are for the benefit of targeted individuals and groups (nearly all of which are non-conformist minorities of one sort or another).

The ideal for any particular piece of work, from a policy perspective, is in reality to produce a colonised mind, a mind that thinks what is in the best interest of the exploiting elite is actually in the best interest of everyone. In this environment education is oriented toward maintaining and developing capitalism (we live in a capitalist society) which means maximising corporate profits and not (as it says on the 'youth work tin') promoting democracy. At a policy level youth workers are not engaged in work that is primarily about promoting the interests of those they work with and amongst, youth workers themselves are 'educated' to support the capitalistic programme presented by those in political and economic control via the delivery of forms of informal (covert) education (indoctrination) that propagate the 'colonial or Matrix environment'. We become agents of the state (like *Agent Smith*) who might, in the colonial situation, be thought of as the 'trusted native'.

Now this is not saying that this is what individual youth workers do all the time. Many of us, literally 'working between the cracks', do what we can to use what resources we have to provoke/stimulate young people to think for themselves and many of us, in our own way, hope that they can 'exit the Matrix'. Individuals can become conscious of their situation and choose to 'de-colonise' themselves (see Ahluwalia and Zegeye, 2001) while youth workers are in a position both to become aware themselves and work with others to spread this awareness.

While education policy continues to support what is in effect a colonial ethos, existing social conditions continue to deteriorate as the gap between the rich and poor widens. Many young people are cognisant of this and while they may not articulate their position in conventional political terms, it is clear that many resist education, even in its informal incarnation (the majority of young people never come into contact with youth workers, while many of those that do take advantage of informal and community education professionals form no more than a temporary or limited association). Perhaps we might recognise this as an effort to maintain their integrity, not to become programmed or colonised, rather than simply labelling them as 'NEET' and as objects to target? While we persist in the latter we are in reality seeking to make others into bricks in the same wall, a wall of conformity, made up of identical bricks, no one is different from any other. This wall is all around us, holding up the status quo and the role given to youth workers to deliver tactical and covert 'hidden curriculum', seeing people as targets for education, causes us to become 'all in all just another brick in the wall'.

Unlike the products of state controlled education our unmediated expressions cannot be labelled, ranked, tested, measured, competed for, punished, or rewarded. No one individual or institution can control this facet of our personality, nor determine its value. Our personal expressions are the means by which we understand and share our relationships with nature, our cultures, languages, and with each other. They cultivate vital social linkages of trust, love and interdependence. To express ourselves, we act and interact with one another in rich dialectical interactions. It is through these expressions that we can begin to know who we are, who others are and our personal and group potential.

Unmediated expression utilises and enhances the path to wisdom, intelligence and the development of talent. It is this that I believe youth workers should be involved in, recognising and valuing people's personal lived experience and their insight into issues that they define as important rather than merely seeking to 'skill-up' target groups according to official recipes and formula. We need to become conscious that what we call 'interventions' might often be forms of 'incursion' and interference – local versions of colonial occupation and the contemporary manifestation of the same in Iraq and Afghanistan – that do little more than take personal expression and process it into the means of exploitation.

To avoid this involves suspending our urge to 'educate' (to deploy the tools we have been given to extend the Matrix) and look to become someone who is ready to be educated by the unmediated (free) expressions of those less tainted by the machine; we become an individual with the world and with other people, sharing the experience of being in 'quest'; a permanent process of questioning, changing, growing, learning, improving and finding new direction (Freire, 1970).

The ambition to build authentically educational environments (that are necessarily dialectical) can only be realised when one is prepared to become aware of the surrounding world and the influences that effect individuals, groups and communities. This means we need to value and learn from how those we work with and amongst see their reality, to become acquainted with their way of being, and try to understand their values and perspectives. Authentic educators choose to change the world with learners (Freire, ibid) not for them or separate from them. But for this to happen the roles of learner and educator need to be in a constant state of exchange and interplay.

If humans can disconnect from the Matrix, they might be able to start to live together and develop a personal and collective sense of freedom. But in the Matrix those who were able to exit the machine were in constant danger of being returned to the Matrix. There are great ranks of professionals whose role it is to address those who deviate from the accepted norms and work to reform them. Those norms include an unspoken acceptance that the state, the government and their corporate allies, will to impose itself on any part of the world that either threatens capitalist hegemony or might, by way of incorporation or occupation, advance that hegemony. The country or group that questions this will be vilified and made to appear insane or dangerous; they will be, by their very resistance, depicted as having the means to create and deliver (in one way or another) weapons of mass destruction or pose a threat to 'our' stability.

The same processes that exist at a global level can be identified locally. The former Education Secretary Ruth Kelly stated at a University UK Conference, arguing for a 'crackdown' on extremists, 'Higher education institutions need to identify and confront unacceptable behaviour on their premises and within their community' (*Guardian*, 2005). In other words, universities and communities should stop being a 'breeding ground for extremism' by allowing people to debate ideas, and turn themselves into a voluntary arm of the Special Branch, attuned to alerting the police of any individuals thinking the 'wrong' thoughts.

Curno (1978: 33) believes that 'community work itself is placed along with participation as no more than a new method of social control'. Allen. et al., (1987: 33) argue, 'Community educators are "policing the crises" even if they are some steps back from the riot shield'. While individual youth and community workers certainly do seek to support and assist those they work with, as a state initiative, the role does not exist principally to help people; it has a hidden agenda. If we did not have such professionals in place as a means of social control would people take actions together and be more threatening to the status quo? For Curno (1978: 23) 'The function of the community worker is . . . to put the lid on working-class action which would otherwise take more threatening forms'.

For Cochran (1986) the aim of the youth work tool of community education is '. . . to involve people in decision-making to commit them to decisions and to generate independence, activity which is not threatening but supportive and ultimately – subordinate'. However, people acting together free of professional intervention can achieve certain goals and be a strong force.

Che Guevara writing on guerrilla warfare outlines how a rising by a few people may win against the forces of modern armies and technology. Guevara's ideas have been adapted by numerous individuals and communities over the years. The Black Panther Party for Self Defence for instance, rejecting professional intervention set up a range of community services in Oakland, California including a free breakfast programme, health clinic, legal aid and education, community learning centre, housing cooperative programme, free shoe programme, amongst other initiatives. The Panthers took the social ills of the community into their own hands. As Stokely Carmichael argued in *The Dialectics of Liberation*:

> *The Black Power movement has been the catalyst for the bringing together of these young bloods – the real revolutionary proletariat, ready to fight by any means necessary for the liberation of our people.*

Eldridge Cleaver a key member of the Black Panther Party and one of the most eloquent voices of 1960s activism defined his political view in his book *Soul on Ice*

(1999) when he said that 'Respect commands itself and it can neither be given nor withheld when it is due'.

This perspective discards the colonial point of view that has it that people can be empowered by others. It sees authority as something that is taken through forms of regard. Influence and authority are understood to arise out of the individual and collective. We are prompted not to wait to be given power – a contradiction in terms that suggests that to be powerful one has to be 'given' power by the powerful. The hope for this 'empowerment' is in reality a fantasy promoted to maintain the social status quo. How are we powerful if someone else is deciding what power (amount or type) to give us and when?

Cleaver observed how prevailing power systems preserve control covertly, whilst seemingly appearing to 'give power'. A common understanding of the relationships between power and control is necessary to allow us to grasp the notion of empowerment within our work context. Although Cleaver's actions were not always moral, nor did he go about things in a peaceful way, his fight was for black people to be able to revive their eradicated identity. He was not concerned about trivial freedoms and rights such as drinking from the same water fountain or riding at the front of the bus, his focus was the freedom to do what he wanted, when he wanted, with whoever he wanted, without the white man looking over his shoulder. The power he was looking for was to be free from that control:

One task that we have in the black community is a coupe d'état against our present leadership, to strip them from that machinery that controls the community. So that new ideas and new people can percolate up, then we can have a new agenda.
Cleaver, 1999

The programmes of the Black Panther Party were their main focus and true legacy. They demonstrate that we can modernise, using positive tactics to meet needs in the struggles that we face today, unmediated by professional incursions. The Panthers, like Che's guerrillas, organised and fought for what they believed in, no matter what the conditions were.

Eldridge Cleaver refused to be kept in the box of his own history. He defied white power. He came to realise the value of listening and absorbing what another human being has to say. He was to say, 'The price of hating other human beings is loving one's self less'. Cleaver, educating himself in prison, also writes 'In prison those things held and denied from the prisoner become precisely what he wants most of all'. The politics of this is the consciousness that while we may not be able to control our environment each of us can take control (use our own influence) to take control of ourselves.

For a person who was incarcerated, and before the advent of the internet, Cleaver must have put in so much effort to get hold of political or social information. He educated himself, which is perhaps the only alternative to indoctrination. It has been argued that self teaching is the only teaching of any lasting value as state controlled education deliberately demotes individual thought and creativity (Fortune-Wood 2000). Even prison cannot hold the thoughts of someone who will reach out despite constraints. Those that believe that *Soul on Ice* pertains only to a particular era might not be aware that many of the same issues that existed then continue to be problematic today; racism, injustice, religion, inhumanity and activism. However, perhaps in the contemporary period fewer of us are conscious of our own exploitation and oppression; the gimmicks of media and political correctness have succeeded in camouflaging our common condition.

Power in noting without control

Looking to empower others has become to be something of a traditional goal in youth work. Our programmes for volunteers, participants or 'clients', are often premised on the notion of empowerment. It has become a popular buzz word to be thrown in to make sure old programmes acquire continued or new funding. However, Weber (1946) argues that power exists within the context of a relationship between people or things. For him, power does not exist in isolation nor is it inherent in individuals. Schuftan defines empowerment as 'a continuous process that enables people to understand, upgrade and use their capacity to better control and gain power over their own lives'. (Schuftan, 1996: 260). Thus group associations are empowering, providing individuals with 'choices and the ability to choose' and to 'gain more control over resources they need' for improvement in their lives' (Schuftan, ibid.). From this we see that empowerment might be understood as an educational process, which does not directly seek to control people, or simply 'pass-on' or distribute power, but creates a space for people to exercise choices; it is achieved in association with others.

For Forrest (1999: 93) *empowerment is a contested concept*. If deployed simply as a tool for increasing productivity or conformity it does not stand up as an 'educational practice'. However Forrest argues that empowerment as an educational practice can build 'hegemony within the working class' (ibid: 93–107).

It is clear that there is an element of rhetoric surrounding the term empowerment but there is also a disparity of meanings. As youth workers it seems imperative that we are clear in what we perceive to be empowerment and how we might 'do' it.

In the context of community education youth workers adopting the role of informal educators can perceive themselves as being closer to the truth and reality than the people they are working with (clients). Here the youth worker (the subject) is the person with knowledge and as such they shape the client (the object), the people without knowledge. This is of course patronising. It is a way of working that is unable to encourage 'clients' to speak for themselves and as a consequence they will stay silent (silent clients rather than expressive people).

Jeffs and Smith (1990) state that:

> *Educators are not there to hijack what groups are trying to do. Yet their invention has to be primarily directed towards understanding rather than success of the particular project in hand.*

This implies that 'understanding' was not present until the arrival of the professional. Here there are corollaries with the colonial context, which was based on the promotion of the belief that 'natives' were inferior and needed to be 'civilised'. The colonised were seen to inherently lack understanding, which could only be provided by the coloniser. Who asked for this 'intervention' anyway? An unrequested intervention is an incursion – the incident that precedes occupation.

In the context of our work who decides what is to be understood or the moment when 'understanding' has been reached? Do those seen to be in need of this understanding ask for someone, employed by the state or its agencies to come into their community and 'promote understanding'?

Curno (1987: 39) argued that:

> These ideas are clearly based not only on problem-solving within a very narrow context but yet again on an assumption that there is something inherently wrong with people themselves, which must be put right by therapeutic process.

So how do we deal with all these notions? American educator Bell Hooks (1994: 47) referred to a '... decolonising political process [as] the most important initial stage of transformation [being that] historical moment when one begins to think critically about the self and identity in relation to one's political circumstances'. Her discussion on the importance of education focused on creating '... learning communities where everyone's voice can be heard, their presence recognised and valued'. (ibid: 185). This sounds not too far from the analysis above of how youth workers might usefully think about empowerment.

Believing that education was holistic and that we need to recognise one's owned lived experience as central and significant to learning becoming liberating, Hooks advocated the *need to unlearn racism and to learn about colonialisation and decolonialisation* (p.38).

In discussing the position of black people in the United States, she wrote:

> ... because the colonising forces are so powerful in this white supremacist capitalist patriarchy, it seems that black people are always having to renew a commitment to a decolonising political process that should be fundamental to our lives and is not ...

ibid: 47

Hooks advocated the need for libratory education amongst oppressed and colonised people as the first step in the process of decolonialisation. She argues that once the oppressed know more about themselves and the circumstances that impact on them they will be able to *transform their lives. The hope that this process provided was evident in a statement from an unnamed student '... we can change the future and so I am reclaiming and learning more of who I am so that I can be a whole'.* (Hooks, 1994: 196).

Youth workers are in a unique position of contact wherein they can initiate this kind of interaction. Professional practice entails upholding professional conduct, professional ethics and professional boundaries. However, we do not need to let the term 'professional' delude us into thinking that we have to distance ourselves from the physical and the emotional interaction with people, because at the end of the day we are still human. We work on the junctions of fundamental interactions. If we make parts of these sites 'no-go' areas, placing suffocating restrictions on what we do, how will we know what can be achieved by overstepping the limits? This is the point at which professional judgment kicks in; when like Cleaver I look to do what I think is best given the potential consequences; I take responsibility for my own actions as a practitioner.

As a youth worker I believe we should be expected to define boundaries and create our own methods of practice. Our values, attitudes, beliefs, priorities, experiences and many other attributes will play a major part in how we manage. The values we hold for our jobs and the definition we place on our role will also influence how we make our decisions. Do we want to indoctrinate and control the people that we work with or do we want to 'socialise knowledge', learn from those we work with, creating with them the means for them and us to become mutually empowering people, eager to engage in discovery and seek out what is true for ourselves?

We are urged to use 'caring', 'friendly', 'fair', and generally sensitive approaches but at the same time we are tasked to maintain order and uphold the status quo. This inevitably creates ethical and moral dilemmas for us. Rather than unquestioningly following of codes and rules would it be more creative and effective for practitioners to approach these quandaries differently. This would involve constantly analysing action, questioning interventions (and even the notion of intervention) while being aware of the values underpinning our decisions. We would also need to take account of the uniqueness of every situation, context and environment, using our experience, our personal and professional background. This is the stuff of professional judgment – there is no handbook that will show you how to develop it or use it. That will always be done in association with others and the nature of things.

The Matrix, like the colonial society, upholds hiding the truth, denying choice and maintaining control. These environments oppress the mind, body and spirit of people. From the point of view of Eldridge Cleaver and the Black Panthers for example, education, acting through the structure of a corrupt and oppressive society, can be seen as little more than a form of indoctrination, designed to strengthen that society, whilst seemingly appearing to give power.

However, empowerment can be achieved as a multi-dimensional social process that might be used for people to gain control over their lives. One important implication in this definition of empowerment is that individual and community are fundamentally connected.

Youth work is an inherently political activity. Lack of appreciation of this has created confusion within the field but external bodies have created and developed issue based work alongside the manipulation of funding and targeted objectives. It is time that youth workers reanalysed their role and gained some clarity about the political agenda they are trained and employed to promote. While many of our questions may not have one 'right' answer, or even an 'answer' at all, the very processes of sharing ideas and perspectives paves the way for innumerable new understandings and insights and maybe the empowerment of ourselves.

Questioning leads us to forsake ready made ideas and products and to embark on a discovery of the mysteries of life, of the world around us, of ourselves. This involves a profound respect for the 'unknown' which not only builds our immunity against the propaganda machine (we stop looking to it for all the answers), but it also reawakens our imaginations, our sense of wonder, and our faith in dynamic possibilities.

Imperialism is everywhere around us today – not only in the obvious places, in the Iraqi quagmire and the Foreign Office, but in less obvious locations too – in repressive policing and the surveillance state, in stereotypes about black people and Muslims, in immigration 'controls' and deportation, in the dominance of instrumental reason and the devaluing of nature, in a western 'standard of living' built on unfair trade and global dependency of the process and products of greed.

But if imperialism is everywhere, then so is the struggle against it. The struggle is therefore not just about decolonising Iraq, but also about decolonising our society, our minds, and our ways of seeing. In the end, all walls fall!

Bibliography

Ahluwalia, P. and Zegeye, A. (2001) Frantz Fanon and Steve Biko: Towards Liberation. *Social Identities: Journal for the Study of Race, Nation and Culture*, 7: 3, 455–69.

Allen, G. et al. (Eds.) (1987) *Community Education: An Agenda for Educational Reform*. Milton Keynes: Open University Press.

Bremer, J. and Moschzisker, M. (1971) *The School Without Walls, Philadelphia's Parkway Programme*. New York: Holt, Rinehart and Winston.

Carmichael, S. (1966) *Black Power*. YMCA Library.

Chomsky, N. (2000) *Chomsky on Miseducation*. edited by Macedo, D. Boston: Rowman and Littlefield.

Cleaver, E. (1999) *Soul on Ice*. Delta.

Cochran, A. (1986) Community Politics and Democracy. In Holde, D. and Pollitt, C. (Eds) *New Forms of Democracy*. Sage.

Curno, P. (1978) *Political Issues and Community Work. Community Work 4*. London: Routledge and Kegan Paul.

Forrest, D.W. (1999) Education and Empowerment: Towards Untested Feasibility. *Community Development Journal*, 34: 2, 93–107.

Fortune-Wood, J. (2000) *Doing it Their Way: Home-based Education and Autonomous Learning*. Educational Heretics Press

Foster, A. (2005) *Realising the Potential: A Review of the Future Role of Further Education Colleges*.

Freire, P. (1970) *Pedagogy of the Oppressed*. New York: Continuum.

Guevara, C. (2002) *Theories of Guerrilla Warfare*. YMCA Library.

Guevara, C. (1967) *Che Guevara Speaks. Selected Speeches and Writing.* London: Pathfinder.

Hoghughi, M. (1983) *The Delinquent: Directions for Social Control.* Great Britain: Burnett.

Hooks, B. (1994) *Teaching to Transgress: Education as the Practice of Freedom.* New York: Routledge.

Illich, I. (1970) *Deschooling Society.* New York: Harper and Row.

Jeffs, T. and Smith, M. (1990) *Using Informal Education.* Open University Press, Milton Keynes.

Orwell, G. (1949) *Nineteen Eighty-Four.* Secker and Warburg.

Purdy, B. and Neill, A.S. (1997) *Bringing Happiness to Some Few Children.* Nottingham: Educational Heretics Press.

Schuftan, C. (1996) *The community development dilemma: What is really empowering?* Community Development Journal Vol. 31 No. 3, p. 260–4

The Independent (11th June 2006) *Just this once, I wish George Bush had kept his promises.*

Transforming Youth Work: Resourcing Excellent Youth Services. (2002) Department for Education and Skills

The Matrix (1999) Wachowski Bros.

Weber, M. (1946). From Weber, M., Gerth, H.H. and Mills, C.W. (Eds.). New York: Oxford University Press.

Journeying together
Growing youth work and youth workers in local communities
Edited by Alan Rogers and Mark K Smith

This accessible text explores a way of working, tested over 21 years in a UK-wide initiative, to grow youth work by supporting individuals to train professionally, while working in community-based organizations . . . and through this investment in people, to create lasting impact within communities.

It is based on the 'Youth or Adult?' initiative, run by The Rank Foundation with YMCA George Williams College. It is founded on the belief that there is good in us all. This starting point makes change possible, and is backed up by the view that:

• Young people are members of communities – now, not at some point in the future.
• Their voices must be heard, for the benefit of all.
• There are leaders in the making amongst them.

978-1-905541-54-6.

Essays in the history of youth and community work
Discovering the past
Edited by Ruth Gilchrist, Tony Jeffs, Jean Spence and Joyce Walker

'Dedicated to unravelling the many past aspects of youth and community work and providing an anchor for contemporary practice . . . The mix of contributions . . . range from narrative reflection to more conceptual and philosophical analysis . . . focus on both influential people and projects and movements . . . They engage with the wider politics and religion that influenced the development of youth and community work.'

Howard Williamson in Youth Work Now

978-1-905541-45-4.

Youth work process, product and practice
Creating an authentic curriculum in work with young people
By Jon Ord

'Great overviews of the essential elements for good youth work, participation and power, relationships and group work, choice and
voluntary participation, methods and experimental learning. So much is missed if we do youth work for outcomes' sake alone.'

Youthwork

Ord suggests that: 'Youth work cannot defend itself against erroneous and rival conceptions of practice unless it can sufficiently articulate its own. Through providing a **framework for the creation of authentic curricula for youth work . . .** this book offers one of the means by which individual workers, services and the profession as a whole can promote its unique educational practice.'

978-1-905541-11-9.

Young people in post-conflict Northern Ireland
The past cannot be changed, but the future can be developed
Edited by Dirk Schubotz and Paula Devine

Covers not just what we expect to hear when NI is being discussed: violence, sectarianism, faith-segregated schooling, cross-community contact, politics, the peace process. But also: inward migration, mental health, suicide, bullying, pupil participation, sexual health, poverty, class, and how best to find out about these things in robust ways that involve young people in shaping the process.

978-1-905541-34-8.

Just like a journalist
Helping young people to get involved with newsletters and newspapers
By Suzy Bender with illustrations by Lyn Davies
'A clearly written introduction to all the basic issues to be addressed when looking to either produce your own newsletter or to get your material published elsewhere. Youth workers ought to be comfortable with and skilled at both these kinds of involvement. The agenda around promoting young people's voice and influence, and the related issue of combating the negative representation of young people, is compromised if they and those that support them are unable to engage with the media . . .'
Tim Burke in Youth Work Now

978-1-905541-46-1.

Working with Black young people
Edited by Momodou Sallah and Carlton Howson
'Raises illuminating and critical policy and practice questions for policy makers, practitioners and academics alike.'
The Howard Journal
'Provides appropriate facts and figures to highlight current issues, concerns and events . . . practitioners, students and trainers should all find something useful.'
Youth Work Now
'Addresses relevant topics with **academic rigour and passion**. A publication such as this has been long overdue . . . **a key text**'
BJSW

978-1-905541-14-0.

Mixed-up kids?
Race, identity and social order
By Tina G. Patel
'An excellent book . . . very readable . . . presents some original and thought-provoking ideas . . . a great resource.'
Adoption & Fostering
'Looks at how increasing numbers of children are growing up in mixed-race families and the influence this has on their lives.'
Youth Work Now

978-1-905541-38-6.

Who am I? Who are you?
Ideas and activities to explore both your and young people's assumptions, beliefs and prejudices
By Jenny Nemko
'With its equilibrium of philosophy and scope for creative ideas, offers necessary breadth to produce good youth work practice, enabling young people to make informed choices and explore their own values, attitudes and spirituality.'
Young People Now
'The author tackles this huge subject matter in a thought-provoking, concise manner, while not shying away from vital topics and questions.'
Youth & Policy

978-1-903855-93-5.